WHEN IN DOUBT, DELETE IT!

36 Life-Changing Edits to Add More Clarity, Success, and Joy in Your Life

To Steve!
Look for moments of joy and
gratitude in each day —
Chellie Phelps

CHELLIE W. PHILLIPS

Endorsements

The journey to ensure others see your potential can be quite frustrating. Chellie helps you unlock your highest potential faster and easier. With the Life Edits showcased in *When In Doubt, Delete It*, you'll be on the road to success before you know it.

Denise Ott, President
Atlas Management Resources, Inc.
www.atlasmgmtres.com

Reading *When In Doubt, Delete It!* is similar to receiving sage advice from a good girlfriend. Chellie uses her gift of writing to share sound, practical advice that can be used by any woman at any stage of life. Utilizing an editor's approach to everyday life allows readers to realize how quickly we can stop and make changes instead of accepting that our story has already been written.

Cristina Bowerman, Executive Director
Newnan-Coweta Habitat for Humanity Inc

"*When In Doubt, Delete It*, shows women how to love, accept and honor the authentic human beings they are through the process of Life Edits. Chellie helps women from all walks of life take charge of their situations and empowers them to unlock the potential they have within to become more successful in their personal lives and in business."

Angela Dailey,
Owner and publisher of *West Georgia Woman* magazine

"Reading this book will have you no longer feeling alone as a working professional woman. Chellie helps you realize that not only are your struggles shared by others but most importantly, they are your biggest learning opportunities. You will feel empowered to take risks, love more deeply and live life to the fullest, regardless of anything that comes your way!"

Lindsay Bridges,
Vice President, Communications & Member Services,
Georgia EMC

Chellie (Phillips') fun, energized and intriguing introduction to *When In Doubt, Delete It* takes the literary concept of editing and applies it to the day to day challenges of women's lives in a new and refreshing way. Oft times we have heard similar messages in the past about paths to self-awareness and improvement - but making use of terms like 'fact check,' 'add space,' 'start a new paragraph' provides a new and effective way to navigate the creation of positive personal and professional change.

Abby Hirsch Phillips
The spark behind AbbyInYourPocket, provides high energy just-in-time consulting for entrepreneurs and creatives based on 30 years of improving the way people & businesses interact and serve each other.

Chellie has written a book that you can sit down on a cozy afternoon, read, reflect and enjoy. You will find yourself frequently picking *When In Doubt, Delete It* up to go back to a section on what you are living right then. Her wonderful stories make the book come alive and help you see that many others are living with the same fears and desires. I know the students that I work with would love this book.

Barbara Patterson,
Director, Student Involvement and Leadership
Troy University

When In Doubt, Delete It is such a fun, unique, and refreshing way to receive great life advice! Chellie's personal anecdotes are so relatable and inspire you to evaluate the important things in life, and then to do what it takes to relentlessly pursue those things as you work toward becoming the best version of yourself. If you're feeling unsatisfied personally or professionally, this is a must-read to rediscover and reignite your passion so you can live a successful and fulfilled life.

Nikki Stephens
Serves her community as an Assistant District Attorney, prosecuting cases involving low-level drug crimes to much heavier child sexual abuse and murder cases. She attempts juggling a busy professional life with being a wife and a mama to two precious four-legged babies.

When In Doubt, Delete It, is a fun, informative take on finding balance and letting go of the unattainable need for perfection. I loved the down-to-earth, sensible advice. Any woman, no matter where they are in life, will benefit from Chellie's wisdom."

Laura Trentham
Award-winning writer of women's fiction and romance

The author of *When In Doubt, Delete It*, Chellie Phillips, gives us such a wonderful opportunity to listen to our voice. We create our stories with this voice, and each one of us becomes our own expert storyteller. Go find your favorite spot, bring your favorite tea, and take the time that you so deserve to read this book. WARNING: YOU MAY CRY, LAUGH AND LEARN.

Cea Cohen Elliott
Motivational Speaker; Workshop Leader
www.Ceaspeaks.com

After reading over the first few chapters of *When In Doubt, Delete It*, I could see the faces of over a dozen women who I will be purchasing this book for upon its release! Chellie's straightforward edits are for people like YOU who are convinced they have a bigger purpose, who are passionate about their dreams, and who know that they are meant to do something big. Whether you are still at the idea stage, or whether you are ready to open the door of the next opportunity, Life Edits is the solution that you need to get the life that you deserve.

Tory Minus,
Author of *Inevitable Collision*, published by Mary Ann Liebert, Inc., Sales Entrepreneur, and proud mother of four.

When In Doubt, Delete It! is like sharing life's joys and challenges with a dear friend and gaining truth, encouraging words and a hug that sends you away stronger. Chellie has a heartening way of leading us to our own deeper edits so we might rediscover the things we love and use them to write a better chapter - for ourselves. We can all choose to take the time to examine our heart, notice the good and say yes to life! Well done, my friend.

Lynn Moore
Executive Director, Touchstone Energy Cooperatives

WHEN IN DOUBT, DELETE IT!

36 Life-Changing Edits to Add More Clarity, Success, and Joy in Your Life

CHELLIE W. PHILLIPS

Published by Author Academy Elite
P.O. Box 43, Powell, OH 43035

www.AuthorAcademyElite.com

Paperback ISBN- 978-1-64085-498-7

Hardcover ISBN- 978-1-64085-499-4

Library of Congress Control Number: 2018963608

To Jim for his complete faith even when I had doubts.

To my family for always making me believe I could.

To my friends for being my cheerleaders and encouragers.

And to my circle of amazing women, you've been with me through all my life edits.

Here's to many more years of love, laughter, and fun.

CONTENTS

Part 3 – Insert

Part 4 – Stet

Part 5 – Move

Introduction

At the heart of things, I'm a simple southern girl with just enough sass to keep life interesting. I drink gallons of sweet tea, I love my Crimson Tide and Troy Trojan football, and I would keep my toes in the sand 24/7 if possible. This book grew from long conversations I've had with a group of amazing women I'm honored to call friends and colleagues. We met because we were on similar career paths, but our connections have grown as we have shared the ups and downs of our personal lives and careers.

Our ages spread from 20-something millennials, who have grown up with the whole world in the palm of their hands, to Gen X'ers, who still love to get newsprint on their fingers when reading the paper. We've dissected career moves and relationships. We've cried together over deep, painful loss. Most importantly, we've encouraged and listened. We've passed along ideas that worked and choices that didn't. We lifted and inspired each other to be more through our encouraging words and unconditional support.

I'd love to have you join me on a porch swing for a long conversation and a glass of that sweet tea. Since we can't find a swing that will hold us all, I'm putting these words and thoughts on paper so you can share the journey with my friends. Words have power, but not if we keep them to ourselves.

Since I was in elementary school, I knew I wanted to write. I've been lucky enough to turn that calling into a career. I spent my first few years out of college telling other people's stories as a feature writer and editor for a local daily newspaper. Then, I became a strategic storyteller for cooperatives.

Throughout college and well into my professional life, writing became more to me than a task or a job. It became my outlet and a way to express my individuality. I began thinking about the parallels my craft and life shared. As a journalist, I'd spend hours crafting the perfect lead story or designing an attention-grabbing headline. I'd go through pages of notes so I could splash in the perfect character framing quote. Finally, I'd place that masterpiece on my editor's desk.

In the blink of an eye, that masterpiece would look like a mix of hieroglyphics and a mass murder scene. Copy editing marks in red felt tip pen ink bled through the pages of my beloved story.

Add space.

Delete this section.

Start a new paragraph.

Fact check.

That initial feeling of *how dare you massacre my work* slowly morphed into the realization that tightening up the story and cutting out the fluff made it more readable and likely to engage the audience.

The editor is the person who's in charge of and determines the final content of a story. They polish and refine a story, so a reader has no problem understanding its intent. It's their job to make sure the writer has enhanced all the appropriate points and cut out the areas that muddied the understanding.

Beyond the technical points of grammar, spelling, punctuation, and sentence structure, the editor is also concerned about the flow and readability. They point out issues with plot or even suggest different points of view. It's the editor's job to make sure the work says what the writer intended in a way the reader can enjoy and comprehend. It's about clarity and flow. A great editor enhances the story so the real meaning can shine through.

What if you took those same marks and applied them to life?

Life is a lot like writing. No one gets it right the first time. We must get clear to move forward. Editing your own work is challenging. You're too close; you can't see the small tweaks. You're attached to each piece because it's something you've created and breathed life into. Being objective is tough. We all need that second set of eyes to look at our stories with a nod to improvement. Someone who's willing to invest their expertise in making our story a masterpiece.

Editors suggest changes. Change is something we naturally fight against. Plus, it's never easy to hear our way may not have been the best way. It takes guts to change the things you don't like or to start completely over somewhere along the process.

We get comfortable in our writing. Or, maybe a better word is lazy. Comfortable is easy. We use the same words and phrases. We use filler words to take up space. Editors dig out the fluff and force us to fill the gaps with words that create a real vision. The same thing happens in life. We get comfortable. We fail to grow or invest in ourselves. We become a slave to our schedule, to the tv, to the convenience of every day.

When we edit, it shows we believe we can have more. We can make something good, great.

Edits are choices. Edits are letting go. Trust your gut. Some edits or suggestions will come your way you won't agree with. There are times we need to stand our ground and stay the course.

Our choices are building our stories. As writers, we determine what happens to all our characters (good and bad) and scenes.

What follows are 36 edits designed to add balance, clarity, and enjoyment to your life and career. Some edits are tougher than others. Some require introspection. Others require you to dig into your relationships with others.

You don't have to do them all at once. Take one a week. Each edit concludes with a series of questions designed to push you closer to the truth the world needs. Do some soul searching and see if the edit is right for you.

de·lete

dəˈlēt/

verb

6. remove or obliterate (written or printed matter), especially by drawing a line through it or marking it with a delete sign.

"the passage was deleted"

synonyms: remove, cut out, take out, edit out, expunge, excise, eradicate, cancel

The act of deleting can be both positive and negative. The more chapters our lives have, or put another way—the more years, months and days in our lives—the more likely deletions will occur. This can be the heart-wrenching losses caused by the death of those close to us, or simply the growing apart of two people who find they no longer share common interests. It can be a hard choice to walk away from toxic people and situations. It can be removing thoughts and mindsets that hold you back.

$$\bullet \bullet \bullet \mid \bullet \bullet \bullet$$

Delete Destructive Mindsets

If you are struggling with feelings of value, focus on what you enjoy doing when you aren't at work. Direct your focus on another area of importance, and you'll soon learn your worth as a person involves many variables.

YOU'VE POURED YOUR heart and soul into a huge project and met every deadline. The evaluations look great. Yet, none of it brings you joy. So many of us spend time chasing one finish line after the next only to end up asking ourselves, "is this all there is?"

We get so caught up in the process and expectations that we don't focus on fulfillment. Too many of us forget to celebrate our success because we are still comparing ourselves to co-workers. Maybe you feel like you could have done more. Perhaps you're already so wrapped up in what the next project will be that you don't take the time to reflect on what you accomplished. Did you spend sleepless nights and long hours on a project only to find that its completion has left you physically drained? These feelings are common among ambitious people.

Be careful letting your success define your value as a person. If a project goes wrong or you get passed over for a promotion, these things shouldn't cause your value as a person to tank. They should be opportunities to grow and improve or an indication it's time to learn a new skill. When things in life go smooth, it's easy to feel on top of the world. It's when the road turns bumpy that we need to look deep into ourselves.

Dig deep and remind yourself what else is of value in your life. It could be family. Your charitable work could bring joy. Or, simply the fact your dog loves you makes you smile. It's up to you what makes the list. We've got to move past relying on praise and accolades to feed our self-worth. These things are seasonal and can come and go, just like money. It's up to us to find a definition of success that has a deeper meaning.

I spent years entering industry competitions and studying for certifications. I believed that's how I showed my worth as a communicator and an employee. It left me with a case full of awards and certificates gathering dust. The pieces of glass and acrylic never added to my paycheck or gave the true validation I was seeking. That came years down the road when I quit looking to others to tell me my talents and gifts were real.

Real success has little to do with your salary and everything to do with your true value as a person. Is work a source of stress? Did a project fail? It's time to turn your sight elsewhere. What activity brings you joy? If you are struggling with feelings of value, focus on what you enjoy doing when you aren't at work. Direct your focus on another area of importance, and you'll learn your worth as a person involves many variables.

Find your sense of gratitude again. Look for small things in each day you are grateful for. Find people you enjoy being around—the kind who build you up, not those who tear you down or celebrate your failure. You'll learn that what you celebrate expands and begins to fill up your life.

Don't overthink the future. That doesn't mean you shouldn't plan. We all face trials in our life. If you are in that stage now, know that it's not a forever thing. By worrying less about the problem, and instead looking for pockets of good, you'll start looking forward to what's around the corner instead of fearing what it might hold.

Remember, your career isn't who you are—it's what you do. Find your value in things that matter. By doing so, you've defined success based on lasting values, not fleeting moments or setbacks.

One of the hardest steps is learning to let go of something that no longer brings you joy (and isn't that a true measure of success?). It's OK to step back for a while, or even brush up your resume and see if there are other opportunities that speak to who you are now. It's also OK to back away from a relationship so you can take a closer look at whether it's adding more joy than stress to your life.

How can you bring more joy into your world?

Start by having a clear set of values. Before moving on to the next project, look deeper at how it benefits you or your work. Does it cross boundaries you've put in place, especially in the amount of time or after-hours activities that will be involved? Sometimes saying no can be the most joyful experience.

We also need to define what success looks like for us individually.

Maybe success comes from the quality time you have available to spend with family and friends. Perhaps it comes from being able to afford yearly dream vacations. Let your mind wander and see what speaks to you. Even merely acknowledging these priorities can move you toward experiencing more joy. Most of us wouldn't sit back and watch a bully pick on someone else. Yet, we find it perfectly acceptable to bully ourselves internally. Why?

Many women have a destructive inner voice. We call ourselves mean names. We talk about how we aren't good enough. We compare ourselves to others. We put ourselves last. If we saw most of these behaviors in others, 99 percent of us would say something like "Girl, you gotta treat yourself better."

How do we end the internal bullying? First, by becoming aware. Every time these negative thoughts enter your mind, you need to purposefully replace it with another more positive one. Ask yourself where the thoughts come from. Realistically, most of us are not going to wake up tomorrow morning and say, "Wow, I look great!" But each of us can look in the mirror and tell ourselves, "I look OK today," or "I'm doing a good job." Even moving that little step forward begins to have significant impacts on your daily outlook.

The hardest hurdle for most women to overcome is moving herself off the back burner. If you can't take care of yourself, you won't be able to take care of others or function at a high productivity level. Find that place in your routine where you can schedule some me time. That might be a soak in the tub, a new exercise class, or an evening walk—whatever you decide—make the appointment with yourself and keep it. Turn off your notifications. Enjoy some music or an audiobook. Write or create something—whatever your go-to escape is. You must replenish you before you can give to others.

Hopefully, one day you'll get to the point where you wonder where those negative thoughts ever came from. You'll see them as the destructive tenants they were. These thoughts limit who we can become and what we can accomplish. No matter how busy you are at work (or in life) make sure you take a few minutes to connect back with you. Give yourself some needed self-love. By granting yourself permission to do this every day, you'll be a better co-worker, supervisor, and friend.

Want a deeper edit? *1. What provides value in your life? 2. What are signs of true success in your life? 3. What negative messages in your head limit your feeling of worth?*

··· 2 ···

Delete negativity

So many people allow a stream of negative talk to play on a loop cycle in their mind. There is power in words, and negative energy isn't what you need in your life.

IS THERE SOMEONE at your office everyone wishes would take a sick day or week? Do you and your friends find yourself talking about the same self-absorbed person over and over? Or worse, is that someone you? Negativity can invade your workplace and daily life and spread like a virus.

Once you recognize it, you need to identify the underlying cause. Be direct. Discuss it with the person in a non-confrontational tone. Be prepared that this conversation may be emotional. Meet in a private area. Be ready to offer some positive feedback. Focus on ways to improve performance.

Negativity can come from feeling under-appreciated, or from a lack of understanding about their position. If it's in the workplace, offer perspective on expectations, and set clear, measurable goals. Work on the plan together. Identify priorities. Most importantly, make sure you listen.

Enhance your ability to read people and your survival kit for dealing with difficult people will be armed to the hilt.

The first rule is avoidance. If you know someone is in a bad mood and you don't have to interact with them today, don't! If that's not an option, here are some other ways to cope.

- Set Boundaries. You don't have to allow anyone to mistreat you.
- Take a few deep breaths to calm yourself.
- You are in control of your thoughts and behavior. Don't allow them to pull out a response. Remind yourself—this person is in trouble. Most blow ups have little to do with the present situation, and are all about built up hostilities, anger, depression, or some other feeling.
- If you feel you are in physical danger, leave the situation immediately. However, verbally confronting the individual in a calm manner can cause them to reset. Bullies don't pick on someone who appears strong. Don't apologize for not allowing someone to mistreat you.
- Ask questions. Make them be specific in their list of grievances. Do not allow them to generalize.
- Use the nice approach. The old kill them with kindness tactic. If you can keep from taking the attack personally and respond with kindness, you'll generally disarm the situation and be able to have an actual conversation.
- The last resort. There are people who you just can't work with or be around. No matter what tactic you deploy, the negative outweighs any positive gain. Those are the people you need to cut out of your life. In a work situation, limit your exposure to only what is required in your position.

If the person makes the change, it's up to you to make sure the virus doesn't resurface. It's important to follow up and keep the lines of communication open. The worst thing you can do is to stoop to their level. You can't blame them for the choices you make. If you do, it's a clear sign you've allowed them too much power over your life.

It's even harder to delete when the negativity comes from your own mind. So many people allow a stream of negative talk to play on a loop cycle in their mind. There is power in words and negative energy isn't what you need in your life. We find many occasions to downplay or pass judgment on ourselves. You must be conscious of how you talk to yourself. If it's something you struggle with, devise a plan to erase it. Begin by acknowledging the behavior when it happens. Write down the first thought you are aware of that contains negative self-talk. Then, remind yourself of all the reasons it's not true. You can retrain yourself not to respond to situations in that way.

Negativity has symptoms. If you are in a position where you manage people, it's critical to recognize these symptoms. Left alone, they can even include a change in job performance. Do you notice someone appearing hostile or angry? Do you hear yourself making more and more negative comments? Have you noticed other people avoiding you? Or, maybe you've disassociated with the office negativity carrier.

Like with any disease, prevention is the best measure. If you are lucky enough to be in an environment where negativity hasn't invaded yet, what can you do to keep it from creeping in?

Begin by developing strategies to reinforce positive attitudes in your department. Be vigilant in noticing problems before they have time to take root. Make sure your department has a clear set of goals and review them regularly. Include your staff in the development of these goals. Are their pressures you can eliminate, or distractions you can help minimize?

Preventing negative attitudes is about maintaining open lines of communication and awareness. Putting a plan in place ahead of the problem will ensure a happy and productive department.

Difficult people find their way into all areas of our life. Once you understand the root of their behavior, you can find a tactic that allows you to work through a tough situation and find redeeming value in the relationship after all.

Make sure you set a healthy boundary for all your relationships. Negative people can be manipulative and aggressive. You may feel taken aback by the words that come out of their mouth. Don't let the harsh words intimidate you. If they continually step over the boundaries you set, or you find the situation isn't changing or getting any better, you need to look at separating yourself from the toxic person.

You must come to the realization that the toxic people in your life aren't going to change. You can't force them to decide or act on a new behavior. You can choose not to stay around it. Many of us get caught in a revolving door with the feeling that they might change or that it's our responsibility to try and help them to change. That's simply not true. Negative people don't share the same motivation as you. Their problems and needs outweigh any benefit you receive from the relationship.

Being around negative people is a drain on you emotionally. It's exhausting. They step all over the relationship boundaries of true friendship. Set limits on what you will tolerate—from colleagues, friends, and family members. You may be related to them, but you don't have to be abused by them.

Negative people bring you down to their level. The old saying "misery loves company" is so true in this type of relationship. It's a strong person who won't allow themselves to be pulled into the next crisis (because everything is a crisis to a toxic person). They may try to manipulate you, guilt you, whatever it takes so that you will commiserate with them. Don't allow yourself to get tangled in the drama.

Be aware, negative people know your button issues too. They aren't above using your ideals or words against you when they feel you backing away. They may point out all your flaws and tell you others are working against you. Be aware this is a tactic and not true. Most negative people are master manipulators. They enjoy stirring up strong emotions and watching others lose control. It gives them a sense of power.

It's up to you to reduce the power and influence they wield over your life. You control your emotions, and it's up to you not to hand that power over to anyone else.

Negative people require a lot of energy. Choosing to engage them in battle isn't wise. Negative people are always looking for a fight. Save that energy. Focus on yourself and the positive relationships in your life.

Want a deeper edit? 1. Identify areas where negativity invades your life or career. 2. Make a list of negative Nancy's in your personal and professional space. Write your plan to address the issue or to begin stepping away. 3. Try not to be part of the office/neighborhood gossip circle. What approach will you take to steer conversations away from these areas when they occur?

...3...

Delete the idea of perfect

Perfectionists often put off starting something new because until they have the right plan in place that will garner the right results, they can't even begin. There's a fear of failure that paralyzes them and keeps them in the same place as the day before.

YOU DON'T HAVE to be perfect. There, you have permission to forget that idea all together now.

I think it's the single biggest idea that holds women back. You must have perfect hair, makeup, wardrobe, relationship, career… and the list can go on and on. Every day, we see pictures, posts, and pins of the perfect life all our acquaintances and friends are living on social media. The truth is, they struggle exactly like you and me. We're all screwing up. We all have a bad hair day. We all have days we'd like to strangle our husbands or boyfriends. Being in search of perfection will ultimately crush you.

I'll never forget my first big communications mistake. I was working at our local newspaper, and it was election time. The sheriff's race was more heated than usual. I was putting together an ad which talked about one candidate's many years of *public* service. I'll never forget the call from my editor the next day. It seems that when the paper came in, the ad touted the candidate's years of *pubic* service. I was mortified. The candidate was a good sport and later told me I probably helped him win the election because of all the attention he received from it. I learned a big lesson—just because spell check tells you it's right, doesn't necessarily make it so.

We put a lot of pressure on ourselves to be perfect. Fear of not reaching a goal holds us back from trying new things or moving away from a job that no longer inspires us. You've got to stop being so hard on yourself and find a place inside you where it's OK to be OK on some days.

In every personality profile, quiz, or survey I've taken, seeking perfection ranks high on my list. I hold myself to a high standard. I had parents who instilled a strong work ethic in me when I was young. I am a pleaser. I want people to be happy and pleased with what I do. I've had to learn it's ok not to see my value as a person through perfection-coated glass lenses. If you aren't careful, you can end up stuck in a loop of feeling like you're never good enough.

It's OK to give yourself the gift of adaptation. You can put in place so many little lifehacks that allow you to get back to enjoying living and stop worrying about the fact it must be done perfectly to be enjoyable.

In work, think about each opportunity as a chance to grow. Don't automatically start with the assumption you aren't good enough or at the perfect place yet. You could miss an amazing opportunity if you look at anything other than perfect as a failure. Trade the need for perfection for a healthy dose of optimism. Give yourself a little credit. You could discover talents you've never tapped before.

Don't shy away from a new task merely because you're unsure. Use it as an opportunity to grow you. Ask questions. Ask what you need to know. Ask someone else how they did it. One thing I've learned is that most people are willing to share what they have learned. Find someone you think is doing it right and ask them their process. It may not be the perfect process for you, but it will start you on a path to determine how you can make it happen.

How many times have you waited to do something until you had the perfect plan? It's a stall technique. Perfectionists often put off starting something new because until they have the right plan in place that will garner the right results, they can't even begin. Fear of failure paralyzes them and keeps them in the same place as they were the day before. The best way to tackle a project is simply to get started.

We tend to shy away from any situation that makes us afraid we'll look bad. But think of all the things you could miss out on if you only try the things you know ahead of time you'll excel at. You'll pass up all kinds of opportunities. You don't have to do it right or be the best at everything to enjoy it.

Does the idea of perfection carry over into your personal life as well? How's that working out for you? It's ok if the house is messy or the kids dressed themselves in superhero outfits. Couples fight. The flowerbed needs weeding. There's always a spot that needs touch-up paint. Stop trying to have that Instagrammable moment. (PS–the ones you see are filtered, Photoshopped or staged.) We've got to stop putting that kind of pressure on ourselves and those around us. It makes people uncomfortable to be around you. It makes you tired and no fun.

Perfectionists have a hard time letting others help. Quit worrying the way they do something won't be right. Give them a chance. Who cares if their way isn't the same way as yours? That applies at home and in the office. Allow them the opportunity to grow and learn too. When you pull back a little and give up some of that control, I think you'll be surprised at how smoothly things go.

The pressure to be perfect and error free will also take a toll on your health. (1) Stress is a killer. It raises cortisol levels in your body, which leads to heart issues. Headaches and migraine become a frequent occurrence. Stressed out people often turn to binge eating, which leads to weight gain. Even worse, it can lead to an abuse of alcohol or other substances to try to mask the feelings associated with those self-imposed benchmarks. (2) When you always feel tired or wound up, that's a good sign you need to take a step back and look deeply at what is important in your life.

The pursuit of perfection can lead you down a path of depression. That constant feeling of not being good enough will begin to take root. If you find yourself in this place, or if you have good friends who are telling you something isn't right, please take that to heart. Find a good therapist, counselor, or doctor and talk to them.

You've got to treat your life like it's the first draft of your novel. There's going to be mistakes. There are going to be things you wish you could do over. There's going to be moments you wish would last a lifetime. No one ever gets the first draft right. Give yourself permission to edit and move on. It's ok to mess up. Life is messy. It's not a bad thing. It only means you're human like everyone else.

> *Want a deeper edit?* 1. Do you filter your content to portray a perfect image for your social circle? 2. Make a list of all the things you like about yourself and your life. 3. If you weren't worried about getting it exactly right, what chances would you take, or what new passion would you pursue?

••• 4 •••

Delete Distractions

Our biggest distraction is usually ourselves. How many times have you allowed worry or doubt creep in and allowed it to bring your project to a halt?

TIME IS ONE of our most valuable assets. We have too many priorities competing for the precious moments in our life. Distractions rob us of the ability to be present and in the moment.

They are everywhere. Think how many times a day you pick up your phone to check a message and you end up aimlessly scrolling through Instagram, and before you know it, 30 minutes have passed.

It's worse in the office. At a conference I attended, we learned the average worker gets distracted every 3-11 minutes, and it takes 23 minutes to refocus after a distraction. (1) These lost minutes cost workers almost six hours of productivity a day and an estimated $1 trillion to the economy every year. (3)

Americans check their phones over 150 times per day. It's estimated that 60-80% of internet time at work has nothing to do with the job at hand. The average US adult spends 12 hours a day consuming media in all forms. All the screen time leads to anxiety, depression, attention fragmentation, loss of creativity, and poor decision-making skills.

So, what can you do to get a handle on all these distractions?

First, know your pain points. What distracts you? My biggest distraction is probably social media. I see the little bubble with my new notification number, and I want to check it right then. That leads to me scrolling, and scrolling, and scrolling. Once you've identified your issues, where do you start eliminating them?

The easiest answer is to turn everything off. You can remove the distraction for a set period. It's ok not to be on 24/7. We have grown accustomed to the feeling that people need to be able to reach us at any time of day. That's just not true. Give yourself permission to deactivate and work on what matters to you. (2)

Don't want to power down totally? Try placing your phone in airplane mode and setting a timer for a specific amount of time. You'll surprise yourself when you see how fast the time flies by and how much you can get done.

Want to get more real? Turn off the notifications. Bet you're surprised how much stress disappears when you don't feel the constant need to check to see if someone sent you something, or if you need to respond to something. We've created a culture that thrives on the instantaneous. No red circles. No vibrations. No chirps and dings. No interruptions. Fair warning—it's hard to go cold turkey. Once you start giving your full attention to the projects and people around you, you'll be surprised at how much easier it is to get things done. Every text or email is an ask—if for nothing other than your time.

Don't think you can because of family? Set them as emergency contacts and your phone will allow anything from them to come through. You won't miss anything important, and it keeps you from allowing them to be a crutch.

There are also some great apps you can set up which limit your screen time and allow you to see the amount of time you spend on your phone. They can also help with scheduling and keeping you on task.

1. Todoist.com – Keep up with due dates, task lists, set reminders, and more.

2. RescueTime – makes sure you don't waste time on stupid stuff

3. Inbox When I'm Ready – makes sure you don't get distracted by your inbox when you log in to the computer

4. Forest – train yourself to put the phone down and stay focused on tasks at hand

5. Moment – track your screen time on your iPhone

6. Gmail Meter – tracks your email habits

7. Wunderlist – keeps your to-do list in order

8. Schedule Once – planning meeting

9. 30/30 – set specific amounts of time for certain tasks

10. Streaks – app helps track how you are doing in the pursuit of a goal

Take a break. Step away from the screen. Get up and take a walk around the office or outside. Use a few moments away to disengage and come back refreshed mentally, and ready to tackle more.

Before you begin a project, focus on what you want to accomplish. If you feel your mind wander off to your child's practice schedule, or what you're going to fix for dinner, practice refocusing the moment you realize it's happening. If you need to, write down what thoughts took you away from your priority, that way you don't have to worry about forgetting them later.

Still need more help?

Identify other distractions and come up with a plan for when they intrude on your work. Do people drop by your desk to chat? Try rearranging your office so you are sitting facing away from a doorway. Now, you won't be tempted to make eye contact with everyone who walks by and encourage them to stop in.

Does chatter in the hall make you want to get up and join the conversation? If it's appropriate, try popping in a pair of headphones. Turn some music on low and use it to block out what's happening around you.

Clean up your workspace. Paraphrasing from Albert Einstein, "If a cluttered desk is the sign of a cluttered mind, then what is an empty desk a sign of?" It's surprising how much time you spend looking for things if you don't have an orderly system in place. Spending time organizing your workspace will help you free up time to actually work.

You're saying this is all great if you work in an office, but what if you're one of the lucky ones working at home in your pajamas?

It all still applies, maybe even to a higher degree than those who have defined work areas and times.

If you are working from home, you've got to set yourself up for success mentally. Outside it's pouring rain, or it's -10 degrees. Is the urge to stay snuggled under the covers going to distract you from working on your blog or website? You've got to train yourself to still think of it as going to work.

Make sure where you work is out of the line of fire of the usual household ruckus. Don't set up near the kids' play area or in the den where everyone will be watching TV. Find a place where you don't have to move things and put them away every meal time. You'll get to a point you never want to drag it out in the first place.

Commit to specific work hours. It doesn't have to be 8:00 a.m.- 5:00 p.m. Pick your most productive time, block it off, and stick with it.

You've managed to tackle all the work-related distractions, now what about the personal ones? Our biggest distraction is usually ourselves. How many times have you allowed worry or doubt creep in and allowed it to bring your project to a halt? We spend a lot of time worrying about the "what ifs" and all the bad things that might happen. We fear what others will think if we fail. We worry how we'll pay the bill if the next project doesn't come through. It's time to stop. Look in the mirror and change your focus. See yourself getting it done on time and better than expected.

You define what is essential or necessary. If your spirituality and family are your priorities, you need to make sure your schedule includes those. When you realize it's up to you if you have 30 minutes of devotional time, or plan meetings that don't interfere with being at softball practice, you're well on the way to eliminating meaningless distractions and time stealers.

Remember: distractions are only there because you allow them to be.

Want a deeper edit? 1. What are your biggest distractions? At home? At work? Internally? 2. Set a limit for yourself – try going 30 min, 60 min or longer without picking up your phone to check for messages or aimlessly scroll through social media. How did you feel? 3. Identify your most productive time. How can you use that to your advantage in your daily schedule?

... 5 ...

Delete Drama

The biggest problem with drama is the way it seeps in and spreads throughout your life, making small annoyances seem larger than they need to be.

I DON'T UNDERSTAND why drama follows women. It doesn't matter how old we get, I see it in all sets. We can be each other's biggest cheerleaders one day and then turn around and tear each other apart the next. We find a way to turn even small problems into major ordeals at the drop of a hat.

Then there's that person who seems to be a magnet for disaster. They jump from one problem to the next; each situation is filled with some kind of turmoil. They are the perpetual victim of life.

I bet you're thinking of someone right now. We all know that one person who thrives on drama. If they aren't sharing someone's misery, they are creating it in their own way. You feel tense when they walk in a room.

Maybe it's you with a rain cloud over your head. Here's your lightbulb moment—the world isn't conspiring against you.

Things happen because of the choices you make and the attitudes we carry with us. It's draining not only for the person in the middle but also for those living around you.

The biggest problem with drama is the way it seeps in and spreads throughout your life, making small annoyances seem way larger than they need to be. You're never going to be rid entirely of drama, but you can limit the impact it has on your life.

I volunteered as an advisor for a national sorority for over 15 years. Drama was the center of almost every issue that invaded the campus group, and gossip was the largest instigator. It can take a lot of forms—lying, humiliations, manipulating, betrayal, name calling, and bullying.

Drama happens everywhere. It can happen at work, at home, and even at church.

Drama doesn't exist if you choose not to react. If you don't feed it, it won't grow. At times, we need just to shake our head and walk away.

When you become aware you are the subject of the latest gossip, stop for a moment and focus. Focus on how the information impacts your life. Does it do harm, or are you just having a gut reaction? Does spreading more hurt in the form of retaliation help your feelings, or does it cause the issue to grow larger and larger?

We tend to make the problem bigger than it is. A lot of the consequences are in our own minds. We exaggerate the negative instead of focusing on ways to find a solution.

Drama queens thrive on gossip. It gives them a chance to turn the focus away from their own shortcomings and highlight low points in others. It allows them to feel better than the next woman. Put what you hear into perspective. If it seems drama followed you throughout your college career and into the workplace, you need to look in the window to see if you are the problem. Are you the constant? Is it a way for you to get attention? Do you like the excitement the emotional reaction it brings? It's time to look for new ways to get those same feelings.

If you feel like you're a victim of drama, deal with it head-on. Communicate honestly with someone about how you feel.

Remaining silent doesn't fix anything. Retaliating makes you appear smaller. Have a mutual friend serve as a mediator if the level of attack has reached that point. If that doesn't work, leave it behind. Be prepared. There are relationships in your life that need to be cut off.

Do you have *that friend* who always comes to you with problems and issues? Does the thought of having lunch with them leave you feeling stressed out and miserable? Drama forms around a negative interpretation of a situation. It comes from someone wanting you to experience the same pain they have. You need friends who put out positive energy and support your dreams, not those who are constantly spreading office gossip. I guarantee if they are spreading it about a co-worker to you, then they are telling the co-worker more about you. Steer the conversation in a different direction, but if that doesn't work, you may want to consider limiting the time you spend with them.

Drama shows up because people make assumptions. If you don't know, don't talk about it, and don't spread your opinion. It's simple. It's like the old telephone game—the more times the story is told, the less likely the facts are going to be correct. Go to the source.

It creeps into our personal relationships too. Men and women are different. We talk a different language. Men want to fix problems. Women want to talk through each piece of it, dissect how we feel, and then, eventually, work back around to how we're going to deal with it. When we're having conversations at home, we need to be clear. Tell him, "I only want you to listen while I talk things through." If you do want him to offer suggestions, tell him that too. He can't read your mind. Don't assume he's bored with the conversation and ready to move on.

Don't allow insecurity to create drama in your home. No one person is going to complete you, as the movie implies. It's not fair to put that pressure on someone. You are responsible for your happiness. Spending time with someone you love and enjoy is the gravy on the mashed potatoes of life.

Use a timeout. Don't add fuel to the fire. We all say things in the moment we wish we could take back. Walk away and cool off. I know we're emotional creatures, but we need to learn to put them on pause and allow our head a chance to catch up.

There is real drama in relationships you should walk away from immediately. Never allow someone to physically or verbally abuse you. No matter what they tell you, it's not your fault. Walk out the door, and don't look back.

In all areas, you set the boundary on how much drama you allow. Learn yourself. Set limits. Stick to them. Most importantly, you've got to learn how to let it go and not carry it with you. That added weight isn't beneficial to you. Our instinct is to attack back. Don't! The more you dwell on it, the more power you give it. Ignore them. Brush it off, say "bless their heart," and move on. You'll continue to outshine them in life.

Want a deeper edit? *1. Are you a magnet for drama? Do you seek it? Is it attracted to you? Dig deep and think about the underlying reasons this happens. 2. Do you feed drama? What actions of yours spread the drama disease? 3. Develop your personal plan for handling drama when it occurs in the workplace or home.*

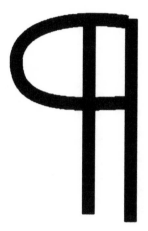

begin

verb be·gin \ bi-ˈgin , bē- \

a : to come into existence : arise
b : to have a starting point

The paragraph mark denotes a new beginning. Without growth, we become stagnant. Once we quit learning, we quit growing. Just like adding the right words or breaking up ideas into more easily understood nuggets increases a reader's understanding, so does adding experiences and occasionally rebooting in our lives.

$\bullet \bullet \bullet \; | \; \bullet \bullet \bullet$

Belief is Your Secret Weapon

Beliefs shape our directions. That hope will fuel you on the path to your dreams.

WE'VE ALL HEARD that what you put out into the world you get back. I'm a firm believer in that. The more positive you can put out, the more you'll get back into your life. I've been known to write notes to myself on my mirror. Each morning when I'm getting ready, that affirmation or goal is front and center in my mind.

Beliefs shape our directions. That hope will fuel you on the path to your dreams. Watch when the words *no, can't,* or *won't* slip into your vocabulary. Henry Ford put it perfectly, "Believe you can or can't; you're right." Yoda made it even clearer, "Do or do not. There is no try."

There's a lot to be said about positive affirmations. I encourage you to think about things in the present, not the future. Say, I am a great mother. I am a great writer. I am a great sister. Then move forward with I can. I can lose weight. I can run a 5K. I can complete an online course. Don't let yourself off the hook by saying I want to. Go ahead and program your mind for success by seeing the possibility as what is already happening. You're bound to see yourself in a positive light if you give it a try.

People allow their beliefs to limit their potential. You can convince yourself something won't work out before you ever even start. You've got to keep the negative from poisoning your efforts when you have a goal in mind. If you'll spend 30 minutes each day doing something that focuses on moving you closer to a goal, you'll be surprised at how productive you become.

Visualization can be a powerful tool to help focus those beliefs. If you can picture in your mind where you want to be, it will help you get there. Be careful, you can create a self-fulfilling prophecy of failure if you picture yourself failing. See yourself completing the different stages in your journey. See yourself overcoming challenges. You'll carry that energy forward and be able to use it to your advantage.

Vision boards are a great tool to help you see where you are headed. You can have multiple boards for different areas in your life. I like to add words to mine. Images are great, but words have power to me. I mix inspiring quotes, or even single words, in with those pictures. What you focus on and dream about will become your reality.

Deciding what you want to do or be is simple. It's putting the action behind the thoughts that takes work. Don't worry if others think your ideas are crazy. Don't let them convince you your life is fine without pursuing your passion. There's always going to be barriers. You've got to move past them to reach your destination.

I love photography. I keep a camera of some type close at hand. Thankfully, it's as easy as carrying my cell phone now. When you look through that lens, that's the world at that moment. You're recording the colors, the shapes, the images, and the people. You add filters to get the perfect shading or the right reflection. Your belief becomes your lens. What you see is what shapes you.

Think of yourself as a brand. Your brand is unique and reflects your personality. It's the first impression someone has of you. Think about your unique style and personality. What are your personal values? Do you have a style? What is your personality like? How do you want others to perceive you? To put it bluntly, I urge you to be the polka dot bra in the sea of beige. Your brand must ignite and excite your potential clients, employers, and any other group that matters to you. You have one shot to make a first impression.

We each have unique strengths and sets of values we use to determine the direction of our lives. Our experiences shape us, both positively and negatively. Everyone tells you to make a list of your strengths, but instead, I'd urge you to make a list of your impossibles. Impossibles are things inside you that you want to do, but that either yourself or someone else has told you that you can't.

Pick one off the list, and prove you can turn the impossible into the possible. There's something that happens inside us when we show ourselves that truth. That knowledge doesn't merely stay with that accomplishment. It transfers over into other areas of our lives. I know this is a fact, and in the section called "Be the Best You," I'll share one of my personal journeys.

Don't be so quick to judge yourself harshly. Your timeline might not move as fast as you like—but is it moving? You need to remind yourself not to compare your journey to someone else's. You aren't seeing the difficult parts they overcome, only the finished product. Ask yourself, if you could give up everything else and solely focus on one thing, what would it be, and how would it change you?

That's your starting point. That's where you spend those 30 minutes. Be gentle with yourself, but get inspired to start moving in the direction of your calling.

Want a deeper edit? 1. What are you telling yourself you can't do? Make a list of your impossibles you want to turn into the possibles. 2. Pick an item from your list and block out 30 minutes each day this week to focus on one thing that moves you in that direction. 3. Try visualizing yourself overcoming your challenge. This retrains your brain to think differently and will provide you with the energy to move forward.

••• 2 •••

Don't Let Intention Stall Due to Lack of Action

We judge ourselves by intention, but we judge others by their actions.

I'VE BEEN THINKING a lot about action and intent. You can judge or evaluate based on an action. Intention can't be measured; however, if you think about it, most of us judge others based on their actions. Yet, when we look internally, we give ourselves a lot of credit for merely having good intentions.

An intention is more like a feeling. It's a nagging, internal thought about something you know you should follow through. An intention is the start of a vision. Success isn't determined by what you hope for or wish you'd done. Before that vision can become a reality, you've got to put action behind the intent.

That action usually means something must change. Change can be scary, but it's typically necessary to move forward. I recently heard a great thought dealing with change. General

Eric Shinseki said, "If you don't like change, you're going to like irrelevancy even more."

Every encounter, every conversation, every thought combines to create the lives we live. The inverse is equally true. Every action we fail to take has an impact not only on ourselves but also on the people around us. If we see injustice and do nothing, we are enabling a wrong to continue. If we fail to help someone in need, we've proven how self-absorbed the world can be. We must be wise when determining where our action is focused. Not every cause is for every person. You know when you are being called in a particular direction; you feel it inside; it tugs on your heart.

Balancing comfort with challenge is important. Don't let where you are now be where you stay. Comfort is our default mode. You know I'm right. Think about how quickly you change out of your work clothes and into something more suitable for lounging around the house once you get home. You know once your butt hits the couch, it's harder to get up and move. Comfort is easy.

You've got to set active goals and implement the strategies to get them done. There is power in doing something. When you put motion behind something, it becomes real. It's both a physical and mental cue that you are headed in a new direction.

There's a step in between you can't overlook. That's commitment. Commitment means there are actual expectations in place. That commitment will move you to action. Better still if you add a voice to those commitments so others can hold you accountable. Many people fear verbalizing their commitments, because if they fail to follow through, the confidence others have in them begins to fade. You lose credibility. That lack of follow through is where action once again becomes necessary. If you really want to change, you must put the effort in place to show people who you truly are.

In the end, we're judged based on our action; whether that's how we treat other people, or whether we follow through and finish projects at work. What you planned or thought you'd do is of no importance. No one is ever helped or no project is completed with good intentions.

Before you jump head first into action though, make sure you check your intention. If intentions come from a motive of revenge or anger, you need to think before you act. These may feel good for a moment, but they always backfire and make you look like a spiteful, small person.

These lessons carry over into something more important than work. It carries over into our relationship with others.

What if you tell your child that you'll be at their school program, yet the closer it gets you choose to take a lunch date with a colleague instead? What if you told them you'd go play outside "in a little bit," yet sit there all night watching tv? Your intention may have been to go see the play or go spend time with the child. Your actions speak volumes though. Your actions say they aren't as important as something else.

What if you told your spouse or neighbor you'd help them with a project over the weekend, but spent all Saturday watching your team play football then watched eight more games because it's the SEC baby? You intended to help them out, but your action said it wasn't important enough for you to give up tv time.

It says to everyone that you are more important than they are, and your word isn't worth much at all.

If we want to make an impact on our lives and workplace, we need to realize what we do is more important than what we intend to do. I want my actions to speak. I want to be known as the woman who keeps her promises. We need to let intentions serve as a guide. To be effective leaders, you've got to learn how to follow through, put commitment and action into play, reach your goals, and keep your promises.

Want a deeper edit? 1. *Where do you need to replace intention with action?* 2. *What areas are you choosing comfort over growth?* 3. *Identify your accountability partner. Tell them what you are committing to and ask them to hold you accountable along the journey.*

••• 3 •••

Attitude Determines Outcome

Your outlook will determine your outcome. If you think the day sucks, guess what?

ONE THING I'VE noticed throughout my life is that each of us has the power to affect the outcome of any given situation, even if it's only in a small way. The emotion or feeling you put out has a direct impact on how someone else will react to a situation or event.

You must get excited if you want someone else to be. If you aren't feeling it, you need to act your way into excitement.

Your outlook will determine your outcome. If you think the day sucks, guess what? It does. Look for the good in the situation. What you put in your mind is what comes out. You choose your team. You choose your focus. Spend more time with people who make you feel better and less with those who don't.

Work harder on yourself than anything else. If you aren't finding ways to improve your skills, then you are missing the mark. It's our own responsibility to continue to grow and learn.

We're like funnels. What we learn comes out in all areas of our lives.

There are no *good* bad days. Don't bring others down by pulling them into your issues. Don't be a drama queen. Don't be a part of the problem by spreading gossip or hurtful information. You won't make yourself feel any better by making someone else look worse. Focus on fixing you, and you'll be way better off.

Plan ahead. Be ready to respond, not react. Go ahead and think through situations that arise in both your professional and personal life. Plan for how you will handle yourself in these situations. Know what you believe in and be comfortable with your ability to express it. We get programmed to say yes to everything. Sometimes, you need to say no. When you get comfortable with no, it will lead to better yeses.

Be careful what you say. Your word matters both personally and professionally. If you tell someone you'll be at a meeting or tackle a project, make sure you follow through. If you give false information, make sure you correct it as quickly as possible. It's hard to gain back trust once you've lost it.

No matter our profession, we're all in the people business. If you spend time connecting with people, you'll be successful in all areas of life. The external world isn't the predictor of your happiness. That comes from the people you associate with. There's a quote that says you're the average of the five people you spend the most time with. I think that truly translates over into our attitudes. Surround yourself with those who spread negativity, and you'll find the disease is contagious.

Make sure you get up each day determined and excited about the opportunities ahead of you. Passionate people inspire possibility. That feeling is contagious as well.

Accepting you're in charge of your day requires self-confidence. Self-confidence is the ability or belief in one's ability to accomplish anything no matter the roadblocks. Easier said than done, right?

Wrong. I think self-confidence is a skill you can create and develop. You've got to be your own confidence coach.

So, how do you do it?

The more times you complete a task or mark something off your list, the more you feel like you can tackle the next step. Each success adds a little more confidence to your treasure chest. You've also got to buckle down and stick to it. Even if you fail, don't quit. Look for another way to succeed. Remember if plan a, b, and c all fail, you've still got 23 more letters.

There's enough negativity in the world. Don't talk negatively about yourself. I have a hard time with this one. I'm my own worst critic and most significant obstacle. It's easy to say *I'm never going to be good at* (insert your personal demon here), and then sit back on the couch and let the world pass by. You've got to be your own biggest cheerleader. Get it in your head that you may not get it right every time, but you will get back out there, and try again and again. Before long, you'll have another skill checked off your list.

Make sure you take time to celebrate the wins along the way. What went right? What did you do well? Write them down. Go out to dinner. Get a pedicure. Dance around your living room. Noticing the good is important. We improve faster when we celebrate what goes right, and quit focusing on what went wrong. Unless you believe in you, why should anyone else?

Want a deeper edit? *1. Identify the areas you need to have an attitude shift. 2. Think about a time your emotion caused a situation to go wrong. What thoughts and actions could have shifted that to a positive? 3. Wake up tomorrow and get excited about an opportunity ahead of you—even if that's only going to work. How can you be your best cheerleader today?*

···4···

Be Your Best You

*Once you prove to yourself you can beat the impossibilities
you set for yourself, it opens you up to believing that in so
many areas of your life.*

OUR PROBLEM IS not lack of ideas, but the lack of activation
and energy that accompanies those ideas. Unless you marry the
idea with an action, you will kill it. I see that all around me. At
work, we do things the same way over and over because that's
how it's always been and wonder why results never change. In
life, we look for that one way to make our passions a reality. How
many of us have lists and lists of things we want to accomplish,
and they stay right there on the list?

So, you've got the ideas, and you're ready to dust that list off
and put some action to them, but there's a voice in your head
that says you won't succeed. You need to become an expert—a
self-expert.

We all have a set of unique gifts or strengths. We all have a
set of values and life experiences that shape our thoughts and
point us in the direction of doing work that we love.

How many of you have been told (even by yourself) something is impossible? There's something that changes inside of us, and it transfers into all areas of life when you prove them (or that voice in your own head) wrong.

I put that into practice a couple of years ago.

For me, this came from a decision to run a half-marathon in 2015. I've never been athletic. Never been what you call in-shape. And never had a lot of body confidence. But my journey to 13.1 miles changed me—and not just physically. Here's what that journey looked like:

Dec. 31, 2014

My friends laid down the gauntlet. "Let's sign up for a Rock 'n' Roll half-marathon in Nashville. It will be in April. We've got plenty of time to get ready." (2)

Jessica already had two marathons under her belt. Tessa and Kadra were already miles ahead of me, in both running and fitness. Both had won age division awards in 5Ks. My fastest 5K was 41 minutes. I'd never ran one straight without walking breaks. I was 44, ten years older than the closest member of my group.

I was literally nauseous the day I clicked the link to register for the half. It took me two hours to hit the submit button. But there I was selecting a name for my race bib. I chose sheer will because I knew that was what it would take to get me to the finish line.

Jan. 4, 2015

I downloaded a training app. (1) I made it three days and hit the first roadblock. Sick–throat and ear infection. I still managed to get on the treadmill for a bit, because I'm determined not to get behind. I knew we signed up as a group, but I knew it would be an individual effort. I had to find it within me to push past the fear and not let failure catch me. The finish line was merely the beginning of a whole new race for me.

My workouts continued through January, adding an outdoor track to get off the treadmill. I was determined to follow the plan and make my best effort at the 13 miles. I signed up for a 5K in March, thinking it would be a good test to see if I'd improved. I can't see myself ever enjoying a 5am workout, but I was getting it done whenever I could.

Jan. 24, 2015

I started week three of the training. Fifty minutes was my longest run so far. Later this week, I'll move up to 62 minutes. I can't wait for it to get easier. Everyone says it will. (I really think everyone lies.) I want it to be less painful every day. My knees and hips make me feel every one of my years. But, I still have that feeling of accomplishment. It's never been my character to do this kind of thing and stick with it. Doubling up the training—the regular workouts with the running—has been hard. I made a promise to myself. I intend to stick with it.

Jan. 28, 2015

Today was killer for me. I had a horrible night at the track. Legs felt like concrete. Hurt. Painful. My slowest time in a long time. 18 1/2 minutes for a mile. I was dejected but trudged through the whole 62 minutes.

Feb. 7, 2015

I don't know what's been wrong with me. I cried all morning, and I'm not sure why. I made the decision to meet the group for a long run today. I was so worried about holding them back. Internally, I carry too much negativity. Jess stayed right by my side, and my other two encouragers were right there too. In the end, it was painful but not unbearable. 6.33 miles averaging 15:09 min/mile.

I did half of the half. In a couple of months, the full thing will be in reach. Mind blown. Today is the first day I felt like it could happen. The Mr. Mister song "Broken Wings" was playing in the jeep on my ride home. It spoke to me. Yes, I'm crying again. We're all broken in some way. We've all got to find the inner strength to fly again.

You can feel sore tomorrow, or you can feel sorry. No giant step does it. Just lots of little ones. It's the lack of faith that makes people afraid of meeting challenges.

Feb. 23, 2015

So, the last week has been like a reset for my mind. I know you hear what you need sometimes. I listened to Kevin Ekols (he's one of Alabama Coach Nick Saban's secret team weapons and a great motivational speaker), and he reinforced what started a couple of weeks ago for me on that 6-mile day. (3) (4)

You've got to get that negative talk/feeling out of your mind. You can do anything you set your mind to and work toward. What you speak becomes. Only I can decide how I am going to feel.

My mirror now has the phrase "I am strong enough and fast enough," written on it. The same saying is on a card attached to my computer monitor at work. I repeat it to myself throughout the day. This weekend I got four miles in—each under 15 minutes. Tonight, I deadlifted 100 pounds and push pressed 55 (30 times).

I am strong enough.

I am fast enough.

I am pretty enough.

I am smart enough.

I am enough.

Feb. 24, 2015

Four miles under an hour! Sore as rip from last night, but I still did it!

March 7, 2015

Brittany Shepherd Pugh 5K today

Best time ever for me – 40:56.

Excited.

March 21, 2015

Having to skip days due to work and meeting schedules but loved the feeling of improvement today. Three miles averaging 13:26 pace.

March 28, 2015

10 miles today!

2 1/2 hours

Today sealed the deal for me. I really think I can make the 13.1 miles. I was tired but not beat by the 10 miles. Tried out the Stingers for taste. Worked ok. Ate about an hour before (breakfast casserole). That seemed to be good.

Apr 25, 2015

"
You did not
wake up today
to be mediocre
"

April 11, 2015

Had a 7 1/2-mile walk/run today. Worked the hills again. Did six miles on the hills last weekend. They really work on my hip and hammies! Kadra and Tessa came over today. Of course, they left me in the dust but always kept coming back to check on me. It's two weeks before Nashville. Rolling, stretching, and chiropractor! Sitting on ice packs, and now I have one wrapped around the knee! I will make it through and to the end!

April 18, 2015

One week from today is the half. I'm excited and nervous. I'm alternating between both all the time now. Can't believe it's almost here. When I signed up four months ago, it seemed like I had forever. Now, I'm trying to figure out what to pack. Electrolyte, chews, socks, who knew! Got in four miles of hills today. Kept it under 14 minutes each. Best time for me on them yet.

Printed off all my race info, waivers, registration, and parking information. I can't imagine 35,000 people doing this. I can't wait to get there and get finished!

Strong enough, fast enough—my goal 3:30:30.

April 21, 2015

T-minus 12 hours until the road trip to Nashville. The weather forecast is not looking promising. No matter, we'll persevere. I alternate between excited, nervous, and ready for it all to be over. Played golf today; enjoyed it and the sunshine. Can't believe I'm this close to doing a half marathon—me! Friggen journey through hell.

I'm lucky to have had people by my side through this whole process. Loving me every step of the way. Pulling me through some of them. No matter the time the watch shows Saturday, I'm proud of how far I've come.

But dear God....please just help me finish!

April 24, 2015

It's the day before the run. We've been in Nashville since Wednesday. We did a lot of sightseeing. We'll finish it together. We're headed to the expo to get our packets and officially register. I'm worried about the weather, but at this point, it'll be whatever it is!

April 25, 2015

Left this morning around 5:30 a.m. Ended up walking about two miles to the start. Traffic was crazy downtown. I can't even begin to tell you what starting in a sea of 35,000 was like. Colorful. Controlled chaos. Loud. Friendly. There was music on every corner. Everyone was cheering me on. So much local support in the neighborhoods.

They had signs that said…

But did you die?

You trained for this, but my arm is killing me from holding this sign the past 2 hours.

You're the (poop emoji).

Burpees and running!

So many people were along the course cheering you on. Kids handed you lemonade and water. Bands played. Signs and posters everywhere. Melissa was my perfect companion. She pushed and was encouraging along the way.

Someone should have told us you need to practice using the bathroom in sweaty running gear in a porta potty. You should also practice grabbing water cups along the route too.

What an awesome feeling crossing the line at 3:22!!!!!!!!!!

13.47 miles 3:22:54 min 15'03" pace

I was ahead of my 3:30:30 goal!

I got a new 13.1 magnet for the car.

We finished the day with food and a concert. I need to think about the rest before putting it on paper. Wouldn't have believed this a year ago.

April 27, 2015

So, I've had a couple days to soak in the half marathon. I still can't believe I did that.

Mile 12 became all mental when my legs started cramping, but I pushed through it. Melissa pushed and encouraged me all the way through. It was such a great atmosphere— all those neighborhoods, all those signs, and the music. It all made you focus on the event, not the steps you were taking.

The hills were killer. I'm not even going to lie about that. Who the hell does a Nashville half as their first one? And that whole "there's always a downhill on the other side" is a flat out lie.

It was a fabulous feeling crossing that line under my time. Way under the time I originally signed up for. It's still hard to think of myself as an athlete or runner—but I am. I trained. I hurt. I pushed. I cried. I finished.

Am I done? With running more than a 5K? Maybe. I've come too far to quit totally. I'm not where I want to be. But I'm not focused on that right now.

It's more about the steps of the journey. The belief in yourself. The knowledge you can accomplish things that didn't seem possible 12 months earlier. The idea that nothing is unattainable. I'm still a work in progress. I always will be. That's ok. I don't have a deadline on being the best me. I'll always challenge myself and grow.

To choose not to means we've quit living. And I'm not done yet. (Stiff still! Rolling! Stretching!)

What does my journey have to do with anything? If nothing else, it's to remind you that your story grows with you. It's evolving and changing.

Once you prove to yourself that you can beat the impossibilities you set for yourself, it opens you up to believing that in so many areas of your life. So, I'll ask you one more question—what is the work/goal/idea you've been told is impossible? Now, go out there and prove them wrong.

Believe in you—yes, it's a skill you can improve

Self-confidence, by definition, is a feeling of trust in one's abilities, qualities, or judgment. Many people say you are either born with it or you're not. I would argue it is a skill you can improve with a little work.

When you begin to believe in yourself, you change thought patterns from doubt to a feeling that you can accomplish anything no matter what adversity stands in your way. That belief can begin with simple self-talk. Wake up. Look in the mirror and tell yourself that you can, and you will. Or, pick any mantra that feels right for the situation. Start each day by telling yourself you know you've got whatever comes your way.

With repetition comes belief. The more you do, the more you will believe you can do. Each win or success will build on the last. Celebrate those wins. Make mental notes of why they worked. Use what you learn on your next project or idea.

Don't let failure stop you. How many people do you know who bail on an idea or dream because it doesn't work out on the first try? Grow from it. Learn from it. Pick up the pieces, and try again.

The world is filled with enough people who will tell you that you can't do something. Don't join in the choir. Turn off the negative talk in your head. Each time a negative thought creeps in, stop and replace it with a positive one.

Finally, share the skill with others in the workplace. Catch a co-worker doing something amazing. Comment on it. Share their win. Improvement comes even faster when you recognize good. Quit only pointing out flaws, and watch how motivated people become and how the morale of your workplace improves.

> ***Want a deeper edit?*** *1. What's on your list to accomplish that you haven't married with action? 2. What mindset is limiting your belief in yourself? What tool do you have to burst through that roadblock? Write your mirror mantra. 3. How can you spread belief in other areas of your life? Where can you praise a co-worker or friend and share in their win?*

••• 5 •••

Don't Let Anxiety Block Your Path

Anxiety keeps us from recognizing the small steps we are taking toward a larger goal. It keeps us focused on how far we still have to climb.

IT'S A NORMAL feeling. We all get it. Whether it shows up when we are about to make a speech or it sits privately with us while we are waiting for a medical test result. Anxiety is real. Our heart races. We sweat. We look for a way out. As an added bonus, simply being a woman means you're more likely than the dudes to experience it. Thank your hormones! (1)

Most of us experience mild anxiety throughout life depending on the day's situation. We cope. We practice deep breathing. We call our friends. We move on.

For others, it can be much more extreme. It can be an emotional blanket of dread that settles over them and physically wraps them up, so they are paralyzed to move forward.

While there are some physical indicators a person is anxious, most of them are in our head. Outsiders looking in would never realize an inner struggle taking place. We lie awake at night as our brain flips through page after page of what ifs. We run through every possible negative outcome of a situation. We replay hurtful words and failures from years and years ago. We feel overwhelmed.

I've also seen anxiety lead to self-sabotage. Anxiety keeps us from recognizing the small steps we are taking toward a larger goal. It keeps us focused on how far we still have to climb. It causes us to focus on our feelings of shame or worthlessness. We need to look closely at this behavior and ask ourselves—"why am I getting in my own way (2)?"

Working with collegiate women, I couldn't get over how many of them truly dealt with anxiety on a level that caused interruptions in their daily life. Some coped with medications. Some visited counselors. Others struggled day after day. The causes were varied. Some were afraid to disappoint parents and teachers. Others couldn't see their own potential. What I learned was that anxiety is real and can be a roadblock to our success.

I'm blessed to work with, mentor, and be friends with amazing women. What I've learned is we can only move an obstacle once we recognize it. We all know the signs, and we know our internal triggers. The key is to refocus the negative energy before it can grab hold. Even the most seasoned pro can experience anxiety at times.

So, what works?

First, take care of the physical. Are you eating right? Are you getting a little exercise? We can tackle a lot of things if we are physically up to the task and fueling ourselves the way we need to.

Secondly, acknowledge the fact something is stressing you out. Journal. Get those feelings out. Keeping it bottled up inside only gives those fears and doubts the fuel they need to grow.

Make time to de-stress. Do something you enjoy.

Acknowledge it is important to take time for yourself. We all feel the pressure to work hard and play hard. Occasionally, we need to pull our foot off the gas pedal and press the brakes. That small break isn't going to cause us to fall behind. It's important to learn it's ok to say, "I don't want to." How many times have you told someone "I can't go to dinner tonight" when what you meant was "I don't feel like going to dinner tonight?" Using "I don't feel" can be empowering. It takes away the need for an excuse, it's still personal, and it makes it clear you know yourself and control the direction you go. It's a small change, but it's one that can help you set clear boundaries.

Face it with friends. Talk about what's going on with your circle of peeps. Don't pretend it's not happening. If it's a public situation, like a speech, have your friends go with you and be that reassurance you see in a crowd. If it's not, then knowing there's a group of people acting as your personal cheerleaders may be enough to get you through.

If none of these work, look for a qualified therapist. Anxiety can derail you and keep you from enjoying all life must offer. Don't let it control you and your future.

Want a deeper edit? 1. Is anxiety causing physical and emotional reactions in your life? Tell a trusted friend or make an appointment with your physician. 2. Do you have a pattern of self-sabotage? Make a list of your small steps to victory. 3. What self-care techniques will you put in place to avoid anxiety this week?

···6···

Begin Connecting

When we connect to our family and community, our feeling of belonging grows and turns us into a contributor.

WE NEED CONNECTIONS. No, I'm not talking about how many followers you have on Twitter or Instagram. I'm talking about real connections and real relationships with real human beings.

Social connectedness (1) is simply studying how people feel about the relationship they have with others—from your spouse, to your kids, to your co-workers, and your neighbors. Experts point out the more satisfied people are with their relationships, the better they feel about their communities, and the more engaged they are in what happens there.

This feeling directly relates to your wellbeing. It improves both your physical and emotional wellbeing. Being connected leads to lower incidences of mental health issues. Socially connected people are more stable, suffer less depression and loneliness than those who don't feel they have a support group of friends. (2)

When we connect to our family and community, our feeling of belonging grows and turns us into contributors. Ultimately, this benefits not only you but the community you call home. (3)

The definition of community and what people term their community is changing. It is more than where you live. With the addition of the Internet and social media, our communities can expand across state and country borders. It's the people we feel are our tribe or our circle of companions. We also must work to make sure our digital community doesn't become a hindrance and keep us from spending time on the people we live side by side with.

Being connected means feeling like you belong, knowing your neighbors, and feeling motivated to get involved and contribute to activities that grow the community. Once people are together, they tend to learn that despite the differences, there are many similarities in how we think and feel.

Pulling people together leads to conversations, which lead to action. It's about creating a culture in which we choose to live and work. It is the mindset we embrace. It is a shared set of beliefs.

What kind of culture are you growing at work and in your community? Are you creating a type of environment which leads to high-performing, emotionally-invested teams?

You are building a community. The members of that community know who you are. They know success comes as a group, not on the back of an individual. They have a service mindset. It becomes a dynamic family who lives and works together.

When you create a feeling of value in people, they feel trusted. People begin to seek you out and engage with you. You've got to give them a why. When you do—and when the whole team is on the same page—it inspires people to give you way more than you ask for. If they feel manipulated or taken advantage of, they will give you exactly what you pay for.

If you start with the why right at the beginning, you lay the groundwork for success. Do you celebrate your tribe's talents? Do you have a plan to help them improve their self and their work?

While connections are vital, it's also important to choose the right ones. From your first days at your big girl job, through every level of promotion, and even when you decide to branch out on your own with some freelancing, the first piece of advice most of us get is "make sure you network."

You're encouraged to join the right groups and go to the right meetings; however, I'd urge you to look at it in a different light. What if you took on the idea that every time you meet someone new, you're networking? You are given a brand-new opportunity to make a first impression.

When you think about it like this, every social interaction—whether it's stopping for your morning coffee, your new workout group, or a volunteer activity—becomes a chance for you to make a connection. When you go about these activities, the difference becomes you projecting you. Your attitude is relaxed. You've dressed in a way you are comfortable with every day. There's no pressure to come away with a new client or business project. You're focused solely on making a connection with another person.

Make sure your manners are showing. Don't interrupt people. Take the opportunity to introduce people you already know to new people you meet. It's not a competition. When we all learn that helping each other out gets us farther than trying to hold someone back, we'll be much better off. Compliment people. If you've heard something great about their work, let them know. Say thank you if someone acknowledges you for the work you've done. Don't play it off like it was nothing. Be the real you. Don't try and use words or corporate speak that don't come naturally. People will know when you are authentic or not. Be confident in you.

Most importantly, pay attention. Don't let your phone be a distraction. Don't be so worried about your next hashtag that you stop paying attention to the people around you. (See the point above—manners!!!) Use active listening. Don't make someone else feel like what they are saying isn't important enough to hold your attention.

Finally, reach out online, send an email, or better yet—drop them a personal note. Follow up with the people you meet. Thank them for the opportunity to get to know them. Relate a nugget from the conversation you had. Maybe you ran across an article their comment reminded you of—share it with them. If you think they'd make a great potential client, suggest a follow-up meeting. Expressions of gratitude will go a long way in opening the door to a bright future.

Want a deeper edit? 1. Who are your strongest connections? These may be different in different areas of life. Make a note of who they are and what value they add to your life. 2. Be a community builder. What are your communities? How can you connect with your community? What volunteer opportunities allow you to contribute and grow your strengths? 3. What connections do you need to improve?

... 7 ...

Build Influence

Building influence is about serving others to the best of your ability.

PEOPLE WON'T CARE what you know until they know you care about them. You've probably heard that before. It's one of the most accurate statements I've heard and try to put into practice. This applies not only in the workplace but in your volunteer efforts and your personal endeavors as well. No matter the group you are involved with, you can put influence building into place.

If you are in a position of leadership at work or in an organization, you should work extra hard not to appear out of touch. You can talk "my door is open" all you want, but unless you are developing connections with people, you won't see many results. Rapport builds credibility.

Credibility becomes essential when you give feedback. Are you only going through a checklist? You should be pointing out the unexpected and what someone is doing right, as well as providing encouragement on how they can improve in other areas. If they trust you, they will take your advice and move in that direction.

You can be passionate about a project or idea, but those things don't get others to listen. Your credibility and authenticity do. If people believe you, they will listen. When they listen, they are often spurred into action.

Credibility becomes trust. People will trust what you say and do once they determine your words and actions match. No one wants to work with someone who is only in it for themselves. When it becomes apparent you care about making the team, organization or project better – and not just yourself—then others will respond.

Building influence is about serving others to the best of your ability. Are you the same when no one is looking? Do you promote others and share credit? Do you genuinely care about the people you work with?

It's a gift you should treasure when someone listens to what you say. Before we can serve others, we need to look inside.

What areas of you do you need to work on? Who do you find yourself wanting to be around? Find people who inspire you, and use them as a guide.

Simply because you're still on a journey doesn't mean you can't start helping others along the way. That's the great thing about building influence. There's always someone you can help along their path. Share your steps with them. Don't hide your limitations or mistakes. Tell them the areas you are still working on. The best influencers are those who share their vulnerabilities as well as their successes.

Make the tough decision to ask others where you can improve. We all have blind spots when it comes to ourselves.

For over 14 years, I worked with sorority women in a university setting. Each year, they would hold officer elections. Graduating seniors and current officers took part in interviewing and slating the next group of candidates. One piece of advice I always gave them was to think of this process as their gift or legacy to the organization. It shouldn't be a popularity contest. It needed to be making the decision to put the women who had a servant's heart and a sincere desire to improve the organization in leadership roles.

I've watched many officers begin their journey, but there was one who made an impression. Mary Claire struggled with school, yet she had a heart of gold. If we'd only looked at the criteria on paper—a minimum grade point average—we would have missed a truly amazing woman who made an impact on the entire executive team. It was a blessing for me to be her friend and mentor. I encouraged her to find the balance between her classes, other members, and personal time when the stress of trying to please everyone had her on the brink of tears.

She moved up the officer ladder and became the chapter president. She led the women and organization through a tough, divisive time. The chapter experienced a growth spurt. In only a couple of years, it grew from about 100 members to over 200. Several cliques formed, and each group had their own idea of who should be allowed in, what rules were to be followed, and what direction the chapter needed to take. Her presence and level-headedness were instrumental in bringing the organization together. Her influence was felt throughout the organization because everyone recognized she cared, didn't play favorites, and had the interest of the group at heart. She wasn't on a personal glory trip. In fact, she sacrificed hours of sleep and a lot of emotions on the journey.

She checked all the boxes for a great influencer. People trusted that she cared about them. She presented ideas in a way people understood. She built support throughout the organization and brought people together. Most importantly, she remained true to her beliefs. She believed in the value of what needed to be accomplished.

It's not about age or titles, real influencers understand the need to reach the heart of others. It's not commanding a group. It's inspiring them and encouraging them to achieve a desired outcome.

> **Want a deeper edit?** *1. How do you show people you are present and invested in them and their ideas? 2. How can you connect and build trust with people you work with? 3. Identify three ways you can build greater influence.*

...8...

Think Differently

No matter what problem you encounter, breaking it down and dissecting causes and solutions sets you on a path to success.

BELIEVE IT OR not, one of the most valuable lessons I learned came in fifth grade. We studied inventors and how they solved problems. My inventor of choice was Alexander Graham Bell. I'm sure I chose him because my 11-year-old self loved the telephone. Now that I'm a public relations and communications professional, I still have an addiction when it comes to my phone.

All inventors go through a process as they try to tackle the impossible. My teacher called it creative problem-solving. These steps learned so long ago have stuck with me and are something I use today in my work in public relations, but I've found they can be useful in many settings.

Step one is to sense the problem. In Bell's case, that was a massive undertaking. He wanted to make it easier to communicate over the distance of a mile. In our day-to-day work, our problems may or may not be as significant. Maybe we need to communicate a policy change with our customers or employees. Maybe we need to plan for our annual meeting. Or, maybe we need to get our husband to understand our point of view. Whatever the issue, making sure we know the problem—or in our case, what we are trying to communicate—is key to the success of the plan. The same works on a personal front as well. Are you involved in a civic or church group and need to address a problem? Make sure you grasp the entire issue before you begin to try and create a solution.

Step two is to define the problem. In simple terms, Bell had to figure out how he was going to make his instrument of communication work. He had to come up with materials, plans, and designs. It is the thought process of the whole plan. In public relations, it's almost the most important part of making your communications effort successful. Without taking the time to really define what the message is we are trying to get across, we can spend a lot of time throwing words around that aren't hitting the mark. Once you decide the message, you need to spend time determining what method will best reach your audience. The same holds true in your personal life. When we encounter a problem, we need to dig deep and find the root cause. You can't find a fix if you don't know the extent of the problem.

Step three is to seek solutions. For Bell, this was the trial-and-error portion of making the telephone a reality. He went through several models before hitting on the design that worked. That's the same thing that happens in my profession. What might have been a great idea at 3:00 in the afternoon after that seventh Mountain Dew, may look entirely different after you have had the chance to sleep on it. You may decide your new, fancy, jazzed up website isn't the best option you have to communicate your message to the intended audience. You should look at all the options out there and decide what works best for you in each situation. Involve others in this process. Ask for input and ideas. Even in your personal life, it's a good idea to ask for help from others, especially if they have experience dealing with the same issues. We are stronger together than we are alone. Including others will help you when you reach step five.

Step four is evaluation. In this phase, ask a lot of questions. What would happen if I tried this? Bell went through a series of materials when trying to find the right one that would conduct sound. He tried copper, thread, hair, wool, and iron to name a few. We constantly need to ask ourselves if we are using the right tool, whether that's getting our message out in a corporate environment or if it's something more personal in our family life. We need to have people look at our work and critique it. We need to brainstorm as a group to find better solutions. We need to follow up and make sure we are hitting the mark.

This is also where failure can enter the picture. I spend a whole chapter on failure later in this book. It's a big deal. If you don't deal with it appropriately, it can shut you down. Make sure you look for the positives in failures. Think of it as learning what didn't work and make a point not to repeat it next time.

Evaluation needs to be looked at positively rather than negatively.

Step five is selling the solution. For Bell, this meant giving lectures and demonstrations. It was during one of these demonstrations we got the famous call to Watson. It was where he convinced people and investors to give him a chance.

For you, it may be just selling the budget to your CEO or department head. It could be convincing a charity you are involved with there needs to be procedural changes. It could be showing management the results of a customer survey, even if the answers proved your programs should take a different direction. If you've worked on building your influence and growing your trustworthiness, this step becomes much easier.

No matter what problem you encounter, breaking it down and dissecting causes and solutions sets you on a path to success. Just as these steps work in a communications department, they also work in life.

One of the most important things you can do is look at problems from different angles.

Want a deeper edit? *1. Think about how you handle problems or challenges when they arise. Is there one you are currently dealing with? If not, pick one from the past. Think about your initial reaction vs. the outcome. 2. Identify people you can include in the exploratory aspect of problem-solving. Who would you like to seek input from? Include people outside your normal work zone or close friend group to get different opinions. 3. How does influence building assist you in selling solutions to management or your team members?*

in·sert
/inˈsərt/

verb
place, fit, or thrust (something) into another thing, especially with care.
"a steel rod was **inserted into** the small hole"
synonyms: put, place, push, thrust, slide, slip, load,
                fit, slot, lodge, install

There are times when we need to add words or punctuation to provide better clarity in what we write. In life, like there are things we need to cut out (negativity and toxic people), there are also things we can insert—or fill up on—that add greatly to our satisfaction and well-being.

$$\bullet\bullet\bullet \mid \bullet\bullet\bullet$$

Insert Your Voice

It's not only about what you say. It's about being heard.

CELL COMPANIES AREN'T the only ones asking the question, "Can you hear me now?" Are people hearing what you say when it matters? What about under challenging situations? Are you able to communicate even in an uncomfortable situation?

Think about this scenario.

In a meeting, you speak up and share an idea or a report. Your co-worker speaks in an insulting tone and rolls his eyes. There are several other people present at the meeting. No one speaks up. Do you say something to everyone? Do you say something right then? Do you say it later?

It's uncomfortable, right? Do you rage silently inside? Do you do tell your three co-worker confidants about it after the meeting? Do you speak up later after you've fumed for a week?

What about in more personal situations? Are you comfortable telling your spouse or boyfriend things that are important to you?

It's not only about what you say. It's about being heard.

Everyone has both passive and aggressive tendencies in them when it comes to communicating. Each of us naturally lean one way of the other. It's ok to make the comfortable a little uncomfortable on occasion. Being assertive doesn't mean bitchy. It just means standing up for yourself.

One of the best ways to deal with these situations is by using a technique called acknowledge and transition.

You can acknowledge what happened or a different viewpoint by saying, "I understand you don't agree with me." This is important because everyone needs to feel valued. Then you transition to how it made you feel or point to specific behavior that needs to be modified by saying, "What we need to do going forward is…." (This technique can be used in negotiations as well.)

Another technique is called *when, then, so*. When this happens, then this is the result, so going forward this is what needs to happen. This one is perfect for the situation above. Comments made in a group setting tend to shut down all conversation because everyone feels they could be the next target.

Another way to deal with it is by turning the table on the rude instigator. When you feel attacked, don't strike back. Instead, turn it into a question. Ask them "what is it about my idea you find ridiculous?"

Eleanor Roosevelt said it best, "No one can make you feel inferior without your consent." It's entirely within your right to stand up for yourself. The techniques mentioned above work not only in office settings but in any situation where you find yourself having a difficult conversation.

Want a deeper edit? 1. In what situations do you feel like you are not being heard? 2. How does it make you feel if you think your voice is being shut down or ignored? 3. Which one of the techniques do you think will be one you can implement the next time you are in a situation where your voice is lost? Think about how you will implement it. By visualizing yourself doing it, you'll have an easier time doing it.

...2...

Insert Creativity in Your Life

Creativity requires thought. Creativity requires you to have fun.

RELAX. I DON'T mean you need to turn into the next Van Gough or write the next New York Times Bestseller. Instead, I want you to think of it in terms of what you can do to add more joy and productivity into your life.

Creativity isn't only something you are born with. It can be cultivated. It's the ability to connect seemingly unrelated things. Creativity is about being open and utilizing all the channels coming into your mind.

You can develop creative confidence by creating a set of habits based on what you know about yourself. Creativity requires thought. Creativity requires you to have fun. You must start leaving space in the day for ideas to flow. Think of it as filling up your creative cup.

What if I told you one of easiest ways to cultivate creativity is something you do you probably think of as wasting time? It's daydreaming.

Did you know there is a scientific link between daydreaming and creativity? Don't think of it as sluffing off anymore. Instead, you may find some of your best ideas spring from these mini breaks. Most great ideas surface when we aren't focused on them at all. When we allow the brain to work freely and wander and make random connections, we are putting our creativity to work.

Your brain takes random thoughts, images and words from your memory bank and pieces them together to form a new idea. This is really a form of visualization. When you think about something long enough, your brain begins to make a powerful connection. You begin to see yourself acting or doing things you've only thought about. In your mind, you are making those first steps to the daydream becoming a reality.

Be mindful when you daydream. Start using that time to implement a creative approach to problems or situations life throws your way.

This same process happens when you dream at night. While you sleep, your brain is still hard at work. You can even help the process by visualizing what you are trying to solve. Give the problem physical characteristics; think about things that symbolize it. Make it your last thought before you go to sleep. In your first waking moments, write down anything you think of. It doesn't matter if it makes senses. It will probably be abstract in nature. Do this for a couple of days, and I bet you'll find a connection and a new way to look at the problem.

There are more ways you can increase your creative ability by embracing certain traits. Try implementing a few items off this simple list, to get your creative spark burning once again.

1. Read. It opens your mind to new ideas, causes you to create images in your mind, expands your vocabulary, and so much more. Fun fact—grab a real book. You get more engrossed and retain the info better. Digital reading doesn't stick—your brain is trained to skim a screen (think text, email, etc.).

2. Reflect or journal. I don't mean beat yourself up for something you didn't do. Take time to notice all you did. List your accomplishments. What succeeded? Who do you enjoy collaborating with? Write down leftover projects you still need to finish. Take time to brainstorm new ways to look at the uncompleted tasks. Make a list of new ones you want to tackle. Take a minute and think about all you are thankful for, and what makes you special and *you*.

3. Get moving. No really, move your body! It doesn't have to be a full-on gym session, just a walk around the block will do. A healthy body is a great thing. It also gets the blood pumping. When you exercise, you'll be surprised at how many ideas pop into your head simply because you've quit focusing on the problem for a few minutes.

4. Make time for it. You've got to give yourself time to write, draw, dance, and play. Try something you don't normally do. Make an appointment with yourself. Write 500 words a day. Learn a new song each week on the piano. Shoot 20 photos and edit them. Sketch two new drawings a week. Whatever sparks your creative energy, set aside time to grow that talent.

5. Clean out the clutter. Make sure you have a dedicated place to work. Make it full of your personality. If you're like me, you've collected pieces of inspiration and ideas throughout the year. Clean out what no longer inspires you. Make room for new ideas. Clean off your computer. Back up photos and old files. Get them off your tablet or computer.

6. Be grateful. Take a minute and write down something from each area of your life (family, spiritual, work, health, etc.) you're thankful for. Tack the list on your bulletin board and look at it often. It's a great reminder to have on those days you don't feel like crawling out of bed.

7. Be always on. You need always to be looking, seeing, observing.

8. Be adventurous. Take risks. I don't necessarily mean go cliff diving. It can be something small like trying a different type of food or wearing an outfit you'd normally never wear.

9. Get out of your rut. Eat at new places. Read a new magazine. Take a new route home. See things differently. Can something be used differently?

10. Most importantly—plan to have fun!

Part of my job as a corporate communicator involved presenting school programs. This might be a group of high school students one day or a group of kindergartners sitting criss-cross applesauce the next. What I learned through these programs is how great it would be if we all approached problems or new ideas like these children.

When you see a young child creating, you can tell they are having fun. They don't worry about staying in the lines. They don't worry about what colors go together. A fly swatter can become a magic wand, and Fido can mystically become a fairy-tale dragon.

You don't have to be so serious, yet you can still think deeply about what you create. Children know how to do that. When they are in the middle of creative activities, there is an aura of playfulness around them. As we get older and add responsibilities to our daily lives, that creativeness tends to vanish. Children don't automatically look at the reasons the problem won't work.

In my programs, we've made rice cereal dance in a pie pan and turned soda cans into race cars, all powered by static electricity. We've used pinwheels to draw mental pictures of how turbines turn and generate electricity. Curiosity and imagination are key aspects of creativity. When you can incorporate creativity into your activities, it causes you to remember information and look at it in different ways.

I think everyone should be a doodler. It's a creative, impulsive act most of us don't think about. I doodle all the time—when I'm on the phone or sitting at a conference listening to a presentation. It's the purest way to get at what your subconscious is thinking. Doodling is the act of pulling from your subconscious. It's one of the purest forms of art. It even works with words. When I'm working on a campaign or searching for a perfect headline, I'll jot down words that come to mind. More times than not, I'll see a pattern or an idea I hadn't considered just by allowing for the free association of words.

I encourage you to be more childlike. Don't worry about the mistakes. Laugh often. Watch funny videos on YouTube. Take up roller skating or anything else that takes you out of your comfort zone and adds excitement and fun in your life.

When you are having fun, you'll see obstacles in a different light. You'll be more free and open. You'll make decisions that feel right, and you'll see opportunities around every corner.

Want a deeper edit? *1. Commit to being more childlike each day. Doodle. Take silly selfies and use the filters. Find small amounts of time you can have these moments of joy. 2. At the end of each day, reflect on what you accomplished and make a list of things left to do. This allows you to celebrate moments of joy for what you've completed and sets you up on the right path for tomorrow. 3. Take a risk. Do something this week or this month you've never done before. How did it feel?*

···3···

Develop Your Leadership Skills

With willing attitudes and open hearts, we're each closer to being the kind of leaders who can inspire great change and motivate others.

DO YOU HAVE a heart? A brain? Eyes? A mouth?

Then, I say you have everything you need to be a leader.

Are you willing to accept yourself and others? Can you help someone else do the same?

When you take the time to discover and develop the gifts and talents you've been given, you open yourself up to helping others do the same. If you're not sure what your talents are, spend some time online. There are so many sites that offer strength assessments and profiles. Take a couple of different ones. See what traits continually show up. Then share these with your close counterparts. Do they agree? Ask them where your strengths lie. When you use your unique gifts, you become more confident. Confidence draws others to you, which allows you to help them grow. Leaders are required to dig deep into their self.

Do you enjoy others? Do you appreciate their differences? Real leaders recognize the need for a multi-layered team. Each person adds a unique point of view and skill set. It's not a competition. It's about creating a desired outcome.

Can you develop a positive attitude? We all have bad days, but do you have a bad life? The way you think determines the way you look at people, the way you talk, and the way you do your job. Positive attitudes draw positive expectations.

Leaders listen to their guts. They understand those feelings come from all the other experiences they have had in life. They see a bigger picture and anticipate problems before they arise. They are great listeners. They know no one owes them anything, if you feel they do, then you aren't ready to lead.

Cultivate your creativity. See things differently. Appreciate beauty in all things. It's up to you to get the most out of every opportunity or environment you encounter. Create your own opportunities and create the change you seek.

I suggest you journal. Use it track your progress, long-term goals, accomplishments, and dissect your failures. Don't know where to start? Try describing your ideal leader.

Our greatest glory is not in failing, but in brushing off the dirt, getting back up, and trying again. Every success is built on failure. Can you recognize that failure is not the end? That it isn't defeat? You must cherish each failure and use it as a learning lesson.

Leaders know how to limit their loses. You've got to know the difference in when it's time to tie a knot at the end of the rope and hang on versus cutting the string before you hang yourself with it.

Are you clear on your values? Do you have a set of moral or spiritual values you believe? Do your actions meet those beliefs?

Leaders set goals and make plans. You can't reach a goal without them. Where are you going? Where are you now? How do you move to the next level? Ask yourself every day if what you are doing is making a positive difference and moving you forward with your plan.

Real leaders are visionaries. Be a boat rocker. Leaders cause others to think. They share their unique message. They inspire action. You must be able to move people.

Do you see the possibilities? Do you see hidden gifts in other people? To be a leader you need to dream.

Look outside of work for ways to develop your leadership potential. Serve on a charity board. You'll get some hands-on experience and working in team settings. Most non-profits would love to have you stop in and say you want to get involved. You might even learn about areas you don't encounter through your daily work (like operational budgets or supervisory skills) that will help to make you more promotable down the road.

With willing attitudes and open hearts, we're each closer to being the kind of leaders who can inspire great change and motivate others.

Want a deeper edit? *1. What five traits make a great leader? Why do you think those are important? 2. Who is a leader you admire? What can you emulate or learn from them on your leadership journey? 3. What strengths or traits can you expand on that will make you a better leader tomorrow than you are today?*

•••4•••

Insert Celebrations

We rarely stop and enjoy the accomplishments as we let life speed past. We're almost immediately wrapped up in the next project or checking our list to see what's still left before we can feel successful.

IT'S THE ACT of marking one's pleasure at an important event or occasion by engaging in an enjoyable activity. I'd go a step farther and say it doesn't have to be a super important event. We need more celebrations in our years. Why wait for the once-a-year birthday to roll around? Why not celebrate the fact that you didn't strangle the particularly annoying IT manager before the project could get off the ground? Find the moments in your life that are worthy of a celebration.

You might not want to invite 30 folks over with balloons and cake for every moment, but you can take the time to have a nice dinner with friends, buy a new book you've heard great things about, or get a massage.

Our want list keeps us from enjoying these moments. It seems like there is an endless list we need to check off. Yet, no matter what item it is or job that gets done, there's a new one waiting to replace it. This constant desire for more keeps us from truly celebrating the things right in front of us.

After working with sorority women for over 14 years, I've noticed we rarely stop and enjoy the accomplishments as we let life speed past. We're almost immediately wrapped up in the next project or checking our list to see what's still left before we can feel like a success. We need to take joy in each of the moments. We need to let it soak in that we've made it this far, and we've got what it takes to keep going.

I've told my women—don't be in a rush to find the perfect guy. Celebrate the fact you have your own apartment, and you know how to take care of your car when the check engine light comes on. Revel in the fact you are self-sufficient before you dive into a lifelong commitment. I promise you'll be a better spouse if you do.

Celebrate friendships. Host a potluck dinner with all the people who make your life better. That tribe of people you can count on in the good and bad times.

It's easy to celebrate an award or special recognition, it's harder to celebrate the smaller accomplishments. They are so important to our growth and the understanding that inside each of us is all we need to succeed. It's almost like we must get to the finish line of life before we feel we deserve moments of celebration.

For some reason, we find it incredibly easy to punish ourselves for failures or less-than-stellar outcomes. We tend to feel bad about every small mistake that comes along. Moving us to celebrate is much harder. Many times, we feel silly talking about the small things that went right.

By taking the time to celebrate each chapter we finish, we are adding more joy and happiness into our daily lives. These celebrations motivate us to push forward and accomplish more. They fuel our confidence to try more and bigger things.

Want a deeper edit? *1. When was the last time you celebrated you? 2. Just by appreciating the small steps you take can keep you on the success path vs. the failure track. For one week, keep a list of your small steps and celebrate each time you add to that list. 3. What ways can you celebrate? Each person has their own way. Maybe it's a small or funny item you buy. Maybe it's a pedicure. Grow your list as your celebrations grow.*

···5···

Insert Gratitude (and a little ungratefulness when appropriate too)

Gratitude isn't just about when things are going right.
Practice it more when things are dark.

THE ACT OF being thankful is one of the hardest lessons I've had to learn. You'd think it would be the easiest. It's easy to do when things are sailing along smoothly. It so much harder when you feel the world is stacked against you and there's nothing but darkness. It's not something that comes natural to us. Most of us must make an effort to practice gratitude, and I do mean practice. We must teach ourselves to do this.

You can take an easy step to start. My parents taught me this as early in my childhood as I can remember. You always say thank you when someone does something for you. Begin using the phrase *thank you* throughout your day.

Take a moment to acknowledge people who do nice things or who do things nicely each day. Did someone hold the door for you? Say thank you. Did your child draw you a picture? Say thank you. Did a co-worker bring leftover cookies? That might require a big hug along with a thank you because we all know cookies and chocolate make life better. You get the point. It doesn't take much effort to recognize the small ways people make the day better.

That gets you in the habit of noticing the goodness we take for granted. I'm a writer, so you'd think I'd be all about keeping a journal—but I'm not. Keeping a gratitude journal is a great way to keep track and keep the idea at the forefront of our minds. It doesn't work for me. I have a friend who has a gratitude jar. She writes down something good that happens each day. Then, she folds it up and puts it in the jar. Every month she takes them out and rereads all the good. If that's an idea that appeals to you, put it into action. I'm more of a talker. When I have talks with God, I tell him thank you for the people and things in my life each day that matter or have had some impact. Somedays they are small things; other days, they are much more impactful. Whatever works for you, make it a priority to notice the good in life daily.

Give compliments. When someone does something nice, tell them. If someone looks nice in their new dress, say so. If their kid just had an awesome accomplishment, share the glow with them. Gratitude is infectious. When you start practicing it and sharing it, you'll see it grow.

Gratitude isn't only about when things are going right. Practice it more when things are dark. Watch how often you complain. Stop gossiping. Don't allow the dark energy to over-take the positive.

I learned a hard gratitude lesson through death. Being grateful when someone you love is taken from you is one of the hardest things to process. Unfortunately, no one is guaranteed forever. My faith assures me I'll see them again, but that doesn't close the huge hole left in my heart. I struggled through the death of a close friend who lost the battle with pancreatic cancer and then again when my uncle passed away unexpectedly because of a heart condition. My first reaction was just like everyone else. It's not fair. Why take the good people? It took me a long time to reach the point where I could feel gratitude.

Let me stop right here. It's perfectly normal to be ungrateful at these times too. In fact, I think it's only normal. Life sucks sometimes. We can't always be Susie Sunshine and find the good. Getting a little angry is healthy. It's part of the grieving process. When you're mistreated royally, it's fine to be pissed. Don't smile if you don't feel like it. The feelings of frustration, sadness, and anger are legit. It's ok to recognize the pain, just don't allow it to be the spot you stop and dwell in.

I can't remember how long it took. It wasn't a few days. It could have been a couple of months. However long it took, I began to understand I was never going to feel grateful because of their death. I did learn to feel grateful because of what they had added to my life and the love they shared with me while they lived. I had to tap into that feeling to get through. I made myself focus on the good memories. I don't think the hole every really goes away, but I do believe you can refocus and use it to move forward. I've used both as a push to do things that made me uncomfortable and to become a better me.

There are proven health benefits to practicing a gratitude mindset as well. We sleep better. We have less depression. People want to be around us. It gives us more energy.

In your work life, gratitude makes you a better manager. You network more. Your employees are more productive, and people enjoy coming to work.

Gratitude makes you more outward focused and less self-centered. You begin thinking less about yourself and more about the people you encounter every day. When we notice the good, we are saying yes to life. We're mentally telling ourselves our lives are worth living. It's when we add movement (or action) with gratitude and start sharing the impact others have that it begins to really take shape. (1) (2) (3)

It strengthens relationships. It creates optimism. It adds to our happiness.

Tonight, before you go to sleep, lie there for a few moments, and think about the good in your day. Maybe the barista at Starbucks got your order exactly right. Maybe your kid didn't leave their bookbag in the hall for you to trip over. Maybe your spouse supported a decision. Maybe your parents are your biggest cheerleaders. Maybe the flower outside your window looks a beautiful shade of pink. Maybe your dog loves it when you rub her belly. There's not a moment that is too big or too small to notice. Just start somewhere.

Now do it again tomorrow night, and the next one, and the next one. Make it a habit.

Want a deeper edit? *1. Be intentional this week. How many different people can you tell thank you this week? 2. Pick three people who you are grateful to have in your life. Write an appreciation note pointing out why they matter to you and send it. 3. Make a gratitude mantra. Throughout the day, stop and say, "Today I am grateful for _____." Repeat the process whenever you feel negativity creeping in.*

···6···

Insert Learning

You never know what life is going to throw at you. Continual learning helps you land on your feet and adapt.

YOU CAN NEVER quit learning. It's one of the best things you can do for yourself and your career. It keeps your brain healthy. It makes you a valuable resource. It makes you a great conversationalist.

Learning new skills makes you relevant in the workplace. Working with sorority women, I had the privilege of learning every social media platform that arrived on the scene. I had to keep up with them to be able to communicate with them. I transferred that information over into my work in the communications field. I sign up for online courses in areas that interest me. I'm always trying out new things. Find things that interest you and learn them. Maybe it's a foreign language. Maybe it's photography or cooking. Whatever it is—let yourself grow.

Learning doesn't mean you must sign up for a class or get college credit. Learning can come from many places. Several months ago, I took part in an improv workshop. It's not something I'd typically do. I don't consider myself particularly funny, but I'd been to a conference a few years ago, and the improv troupe from Second City put on a workshop about how the skills improv artists use could help you in the business world. When a workshop was offered locally, I climbed out of my comfort box, gave up my lunch hour, and gave it a try.

What I learned was enlightening.

1. Stay in the moment. Don't zone out and don't assume you know what someone else is going to say.

2. It's always "yes, and..." Never no.

3. Listen. Then listen some more.

4. If it makes you a little uncomfortable, it's making you grow.

5. It's about helping others keep it going. You've got to really work at giving them enough to be able to continue the scene.

The other benefit, a lot of laughter, and I came back to work with a renewed energy. The simple act of trying something new, being around new people, and using a set of skills that aren't natural can fuel you to tackle your usual projects in a way you never expected.

You never know what life is going to throw at you. Continual learning helps you land on your feet and adapt. Maybe your company downsizes. Maybe your husband is transferred. Knowing that you can learn new skills sets you up to confidently face challenges that come along. Life really is like a series of improvisations. Our final chapters aren't written, so being able to adapt and thrive makes you a success.

If you are starting out in a career, being willing to learn helps you stand out from the crowd. You are growing your personal brand. You will stand out from all the masses that only do what is required. With each new success, you'll grow in confidence and have a feeling of accomplishment.

Learning opens your eyes to new opportunities and ideas. When you try something new, you learn new things about yourself. It changes how you look at things. It gives you a better understanding of how things work. It allows you to look at problems from different angles.

Thanks to technology, we have access to so much information in so many forms. If you aren't a reader, you can listen to podcasts, watch videos, sit through webinars, and attend online classes. If you need to be around people, get out and go to lectures and events hosted in your local area.

It's important to grow your curiosity and not get stagnant. Stay inquisitive. Experiment. Grow. I think one of the greatest gifts we're given by God is our potential. It's up to us to fulfill it.

Want a deeper edit? 1. Write a list of skills that would benefit you in your career or philanthropic work. 2. Search online for programs that would be beneficial to you and cause you to feel excited about learning again. 3. Find one podcast that sparks an interest and listen to three episodes this week.

... 7 ...

Recharge Your Batteries

It's imperative you find ways to refill your fuel tanks. Caring for yourself allows you to be able to care for the people and causes that matter.

LIKE OUR CELL phones and tablets, we need to recharge too. We each have a limited amount of energy. When we run out, we feel frazzled, exhausted, irritable, and less like the *Wonder Women* we know we are.

It's imperative you find ways to refill your fuel tanks. Caring for yourself allows you to be able to care for the people and causes that matter to you.

There's one friend in my circle who keeps a schedule that makes a tilt-a-whirl look like it's standing still. Between traveling for fun and work, volunteering, coaching, taking part in political campaigns, and about 200 other activities, I'm amazed she has any energy left to get through daily work activities and take care of the normal things like laundry. We're all different. She gets energy from these environments. Another friend loves nothing more than grabbing a beer from the fridge, and sitting on her deck while she plays with her dogs and decompresses after a day at the office.

Recharging doesn't have to mean packing up and running away to an expensive retreat once a year (although if that's your thing pack me in your suitcase please). I think it's vital we find little ways to recharge that fit into our hectic lives.

For me, I love to schedule a massage. When I do that, it gives me permission to turn off every device that dings or competes for my attention and close my eyes. Spa rules, so who am I to argue? For 60 minutes, you breathe in soothing aromatherapy, focus on the sounds of soothing water fountains, and simply relax while someone rubs away every point of stress. I don't think of it as being selfish, and I do my best to clear my mind of any list that starts forming of all the things I need to be doing.

That hour makes me more productive and healthy. My other quick fix is to lock myself in the bathroom. Fill up the tub with bubbles and let all my stress go down the drain. I read a book or listen to music, and I stay there until the water turns cold. I'm happier and ready to face the next challenge after I've toweled off and had that time to regroup.

You've got to take those moments when you can. I'd say schedule them in your planner. Make an appointment with yourself. Don't think about your obligations, bills, kids, job, family, or the fact the dog dug up the flowerbed. Every one of these things won't seem as daunting once you've had time to decompress.

We have a never-ending list of commitments. It's no wonder we're always tired. Learning to say no and simplify can be one of the best ways to get longer life out of your internal batteries. Delegate where you can. Before you agree to the next thing, ask yourself what you are taking away from.

I also find that in periods of recharging, ideas tend to surface. When you allow your mind to wander and not force it into a certain mode of thinking, it's always surprising to me how many aha moments occur.

Making time for yourself helps you face tomorrow, and the next day, and the next.

Want a deeper edit? *1. Find 15 minutes today and take a break. Enjoy the outdoors, sit and read, pop your headphones in, and listen to your favorite band. Do this every day for a week. 2. How did adding these moments of you time in your day make you feel? Did you stress over what you could or should be doing? Did you find by the end of the week that time actually allowed you to come back more focused on a task? 3. Going forward, put your 15-minute blocks in your planner and make an appointment with yourself.*

stet
/stet/

verb

let it stand (used as an instruction on a printed proof to indicate that a correction or alteration should be ignored).

Sometimes an editor gets it wrong. There are times when a suggested correction needs to be ignored. In life, there are times we need to stay the course and stick to what we know is right.

··· | ···

Remain Authentically You

When you dare to be you, you'll feel inner happiness that radiates and causes the right people to gravitate to you.

BE AUTHENTICALLY YOU. Sounds easy, right? But we all get caught up in trying to please friends, teachers, parents, and bosses. A lot of people spend so much time putting on the right face for the right group that they begin to lose what makes them unique. Some forget entirely! Make sure you let your light shine through. Allow your creativity to surface. Don't limit yourself with someone else's boundaries. Make sure your actions reflect who you are.

I don't know why women feel that being their best self means they need to be like someone else. Whatever the reason, it starts early. I remember being in middle school and knowing I wasn't like the group I wanted to feel included in. It didn't matter how many pairs of acid washed jeans I owned or how big I could get my hair, it was what was on the inside that made me different. It was later in life before I found my group—the ones who accepted me and my quirks and made me feel like being me was enough.

We spend so much energy trying to be who we aren't. Never get so busy trying to make a cookie cutter version of yourself fit that you forget to make a life where you are appreciated for you.

This pretending to be someone we aren't exposes us to a lot of self-imposed drama. By avoiding it from the beginning, you can start a lifetime of celebrating the things that make you uniquely you. So, how can you get started on the right foot?

Don't let fear stop you. Don't play the comparison game. You are you. If you are afraid to share your beliefs or ideas because you fear the group's judgment, you need to look for a different group of friends. True friends accept your differences and revel in the differences that make you who you are.

I've seen many women struggle with the need for validation. We want the perfect grade, the perfect outfit, the perfect body, or the perfect relationship. None of these things impact our value as a person. We allow drama to seep in when we let other's opinions of how we measure up cloud our view of ourselves. When we finally realize how someone else sees us is their issue and not ours, we can let the drama go and begin to live.

My friend Casey is 20 years younger than me. I'm amazed at what she has accomplished and continues to accomplish. I love our life talks. We share relationship issues, career ups and downs, and mostly life. What I wish most for her is that she never let her shine dull. I hope broken promises never take away her drive and determination. I hope she never forgets that being her is enough.

She has a list of things she wants to accomplish, and she wants to do it in a way that honors her family and the town she's grown up in. I admire that. I worry that her self-imposed timeline creates undue stress on her. I laugh with her, not at her, over this because I can't imagine myself having everything planned out so far ahead. I swear she has her 30-year plan all mapped out. I worry her perfectionism and lack of sleep will take a physical toll. I fear what will happen to her spark if she stays at an organization where her creativity and drive isn't recognized or encouraged. If I could convince her of one thing, it would be that there is no foolproof way to manage life.

There will be plenty of times in life when we are confused, unsure, or pissed off. Those are the times we need to step back and take the emotion out of it. We need to look at it as if it were happening to someone else. Would we want them treated that way? Would we encourage them to run to the nearest exit? This is when it's so important to know what we value in life and what gives us purpose.

I call it the *High 5* approach. It's a way of looking at the consequences of our choices and actions, and it works on a big or small scale. Think of it this way—how will a choice impact you in five minutes, five days, five months, or five years? When you break it down, you begin to see if you are remaining true to the values and desires you have for your life.

It's important to own what sets you apart from others. Use these differences as strengths. Don't follow the crowd—lead it. Give yourself permission to be you. No one else can do it. When you dare to be you, you'll feel inner happiness that radiates and causes the right people to gravitate to you.

Don't allow someone else to make you feel insignificant. Each of us matter and have something special inside the world needs to see. You are impacting someone else even if you are unaware of the effect you have. The world would not be the same place without you in it.

This is even truer in relationships. The foundation of that word is relate, which means to find common ground and ideas. The problem comes when a person tries to mold someone into their predetermined idea of what and who they should be. No one is going to be a perfect fit every day. Relationships are partnerships. For them to thrive, each person must accept the differences the other brings. Being committed, but only if someone changes themselves, is asking for failure and discourse. The only person anyone has the power to makeover is themselves. Don't fall into a trap thinking changing pieces of you will make someone love or appreciate you more.

Remaining authentic is tough. In a society that points out differences, it's easy to want to cover up what you see as differences. I'm here to tell you there's nothing wrong with you being you. Allow yourself to let your individuality shine bright.

Want a deeper edit? 1. Use the High 5 method with a choice you need to make this week. What happens if you go to the soccer game instead of working late? What if you skip your kid's school play? What if you tell your boss no to attending a conference? 2. What are you afraid of? 3. Think of a time when someone made you feel insignificant about a desire or passion you carry. See yourself pushing past that and accomplishing your desire. What does that look like?

••• 2 •••

Remain in Control

By taking the emotion down a notch, you are establishing more credibility as a professional.

HAVE YOU EVER cried at work? Slammed a door? Felt your temple throbbing in anger?

Most of us have allowed emotions to creep into the workplace either because a co-worker, a boss, or even a customer managed to slip past our self-control. You've got to remember you are your CEO—chief emotional officer.

Emotions are what make us human; however, learning to manage them is what makes us a better communicator and leader. We've all seen that interview go horribly wrong on a news program—when the interviewee allowed the interviewer to press one of their hot buttons. (1)(2)

Do you know your hot buttons? It's taken a while for me to identify mine. I can feel myself getting hot under the collar when I feel like I am being unappreciated or taken advantage of. I also feel annoyed when I think other people don't respect hard deadlines or the work that goes into projects.

I will take a lot. I bottle things up. Then suddenly, I blow up over something relatively small. What I've learned over the years is if I'd have addressed the real issues much earlier, I could have prevented the situation from escalating. The feeling of being undervalued or feeling that my time wasn't important was very real. I just failed to communicate it in a way that solved the issue.

If it's not someone who routinely pushes my buttons, I've learned to look for a positive. Maybe they dumped a project on you at the last minute because you've excelled all the other times. They felt they could count on you to get it done. That small glimmer can help you move past the frustration. You can give them a break. They probably didn't do it to annoy you deliberately.

Anger is generally a mask for deeper feelings. Anger is something that builds. If you learn to recognize it early, you can address the root causes before you blow. Does your boss missing deadlines add undue stress on you? Try adjusting your due date to compensate for the problem before it occurs.

Anger can also become a habit. Anger is a lot easier for us to express than other feelings. You can tell someone you're mad much easier than you can tell them you feel undervalued. Anger is a convenient cover for other emotions we choose not to deal with or act on. Anger isn't always bad. It can be a powerful motivator. It's filled with energy and can spur us to make a change.

Disappointment is an emotion which effects work more than any other one. Disappointment leads to low energy, morale issues, and makes you ok with the status quo. If you get passed over for promotions or project leads, it can be hard to get excited about coming to work every day. It's up to you to find those small glimmers that make your day better. Maybe you can learn a new skill that will show your manager you have more to contribute. Perhaps you can volunteer for an organization and gain that sense of contribution you desire.

What if you aren't the one who is emotional? What if you are the one dealing with an emotional co-worker? Sometimes you need to let them vent and listen to what they are really saying. Don't interrupt. Ask questions that force them to provide details and thoughts. Don't let them interrupt you when you respond. If they can't calm down, tell them to take a pause. Let them know the conversation can't continue in the current manner. Take a break if necessary and address it again later.

If you are the emotional one, take time to identify what it is you are feeling and why. Change your self-talk (is it really true that no one cares how it impacts you, here we go again, no one listens). Affirm your rights; you are in control of you. Walk away. Take a breath. Then, be strategic about your communications. Address the real issue, offer suggestions, or ask for help.

By taking the emotion down a notch, you are establishing more credibility as a professional.

The biggest lessons I've learned are—

1. You get to choose how you react.

2. Try not to react in the moment.

3. Keep your composure. Breathe slowly, maintain eye contact, and respectfully disagree if you need to.

4. Excuse yourself. It's ok to tell someone you need to take some time before you continue the discussion. Set a time to come back and address the issue at hand once you've had time to collect your thoughts.

Want a deeper edit? 1. Describe the last time you let emotion get the best of you. It can be either in a personal or professional setting. Look at what set you off? Get to the heart of what caused you to react. 2. Identify your triggers and make a plan to address that going forward. 3. How do you feel when someone else is the emotional one? What is your plan of attack the next time you are in that situation?

...3...

Remain Balanced

It doesn't really matter if my plate has more on it than yours; it's all about choices.

DO YOU HAVE those days where you'd like to stay under the covers and not face the office? We all do. The key is finding that balance where those days are few and far between. We all have a different idea of what that looks like. That's OK. The key is recognizing what it looks like to you and make sure you keep that picture in mind.

Remaining balanced is about making sure you aren't pushed or pulled too far in one direction or the other. It doesn't matter if my plate has more on it than yours; it's all about our personal choices. It doesn't matter if you're a blogger, stay-at-home mom, or a nine-to-fiver. It's important to prioritize things in your life to make sure every area—spiritual, physical, and emotional—are equally represented. That doesn't mean you must have the same amount of time devoted to each category each day, only that you achieve an overall balance in those areas.

This translates over into the workforce and the people we manage.

Are your employees giving their best self on most days? If not, you need to figure out what is out of balance. Are they overwhelmed? Are they bored? Either is exactly as big of a problem as the other.

You need to help your team find focus. Sometimes when we dump more and more ideas and projects into the mix, it becomes hard to make any of them a success. People need help in narrowing down what is essential. Having defined tasks comforts people, and it allows them to concentrate on achieving a specific goal. Others thrive on a challenge.

Do you always say yes to everything? Sometimes you need to say no. Not taking on additional projects when you are already under stress is ok. You must be gentle with you. Saying no leads to better yeses down the road.

Finally, we all need an attitude adjustment at times. What happens when we let someone else affect our attitude? It normally only takes seconds for that to happen. You've got to remember that you get to choose how you respond.

When you take time to choose your team and your focus wisely, you're setting yourself up for success. Balance comes from spending more minutes with people who make you feel better and less with those who don't. That's true both at work and in your personal life.

Finding balance is a problem for a lot of people. If you Google "finding balance in life" you'll get over 50,000,000 results. So, where do you even start?

First, prioritize. Remember earlier when you defined what true success looked like to you? This is where it comes full circle. When you know what matters to you, you will keep the important things in front of you. I don't think your balance point remains the same. There will be times when you must give more time to work than family. That works if you make sure it's not an everyday expectation (think the *High 5* formula). The pendulum swings back and forth and so do our obligations. The balance comes in making sure the weight doesn't get frozen on one side or the other.

Set goals. Break them into short-term and long-term plans. That will make them more manageable, and you'll get to celebrate each step of the way.

Make balance a choice. It's ok to say no sometimes. Assess where you are now and determine what you need to cut to make time for your priorities.

Balance is about making time for both internal (the you things—emotions, health, spirituality, mind) and the external (work, friends, family). It's not about choosing one over the other. Be honest with yourself about areas you've been neglecting. Reflect along the way to make sure your new plan addresses your concerns.

Want a deeper edit? 1. Where do you need more balance in life? Is there an area you've been neglecting? 2. Reflect on what you want to accomplish and set goals that will get you there. 3. It's empowering to take care of yourself. Making you a priority is a good thing. Be conscious not to allow guilt or negative self-talk derail your efforts. If you experience this, think about where those feelings are coming from and why they affect you so profoundly.

•••4•••

Embrace Your Vision

I don't think our original vision has to be our only vision.

WITH ANY WRITING project, the key is to have a vision. What feelings will your story evoke? What questions will it answer? What story do you want to tell? Like with your written word, people need to hear your story and message. What you believe to be true is what you will live.

It's important we choose to see the possibilities before us. I don't think our original vision has to be our only vision. If you apply the other tactics you find throughout this book, you'll notice a lot of growth and change happening with each passing year. If you are lucky enough to know right from the start where you're going and how you'll end up there—yeah you! I'm glad there are folks out there like you.

For me, it's been a game of stepping stones. I knew at an early age I loved words. What I didn't realize was that sharing my struggles and what I've learned along the way would become a vital part of who I am. Mentoring and working with collegiate women gave me the joy and energy to push myself further. I've learned so much more about myself through my efforts to help guide the sorority women and young professionals I've worked with as they searched for their path. They've caused me to dig deep into my decisions so that I could share my why with them. I've also looked at choices I wished I had made differently and analyzed why I went down that road.

Most writers outline in some form or fashion. I start with a traditional paper outline, but as my projects progress, I move to large sticky note type paper that covers my wall. I use bright colored markers for different segments or areas. I even add smaller sticky notes to the pages if new things crop up, and I'm out of room. The visioning process looks very similar to me. I know the core pieces and have some forward-thinking areas, but I need the parts that connect the dots.

My favorite part of the process is closing my eyes and dreaming of all the things my future can be. I'm a big believer in seeing yourself where you want to go. I've pictured myself on stage talking with groups. I've seen myself encouraging a friend. I've watched sorority women achieve milestones that a couple of years prior they didn't have enough faith in themselves to see. These things make up who I am. I'm a writer and an encourager; I'm a dreamer and a believer.

Moving that vision forward requires us to take stock of the skills and connections we possess. I have a journalism degree and worked in both print and radio before settling in a corporate public relations role. I've taken workshops in cybersecurity and social media. I've been certified in social media marketing. I've volunteered to mentor and advise. I've signed up for online courses that interested me, like public speaking and blogging for business. Everything I do, I do with my end goal in mind. It's up to me to fuel that desire and provide myself with the tools necessary to reach my goals. One cautionary tale—don't get so caught up in learning that you fail to do anything with the information. Don't leave your gifts sitting on a shelf collecting dust. Hit the start button and get moving.

Like any writer, we need deadlines. I'm a proverbial procrastinator. I'll start tons of projects, but unless I set a time limit, those projects may never be finished. I think it's part of the DNA of a newspaper reporter. I also need to make sure I'm not the only one who knows that deadline. I need my accountability partners. These are the people I share my dreams and goals with. They are the people who will ask me, "Where are you on your journey?" They are my GPS. The ones who will tell me make an immediate U-turn or help me find a detour if I run across a roadblock along the way.

I'm part of a women's executive coaching group. We get together once a month and talk about our lives and careers. During one of our last sessions, we discussed the different ways people set goals. Some people like to set small goals and attain them. Then, add a new goal that's a little farther down the road. Once they reach it, they add another and continue repeating the process.

Others like to set a stretch goal. That's one you know is going to take extra effort to reach. It's just a little bit out of your comfort zone. Deep down inside, you know you can achieve it but, it's going to force you to work hard to get there.

Then there are those of us who set B-HAG goals. Those are the big, hairy, audacious goals. You really have no idea how long or if you will get there. You thrive on that challenge. The important thing is if you set these goals, you have the mindset that you're farther along than you were last year, and you'll just keep trying. If your mindset is one of if you don't make it over the finish line you've failed, you need to be careful how you set your goals so you don't get stalled.

What we learned is that most of us are a combination of these types. We love big picture goals. We also need some smaller stretch goals to check off along the journey. As long as we are moving forward, it's ok.

That doesn't mean you must reach your goal tomorrow. Don't get so obsessed on the future you forget to live today. I'm a firm believer in living each day to the fullest. We're only guaranteed the one we are in at this moment. You simply must keep pressing forward.

Carolyn was like that. I lost her to pancreatic cancer a few years ago. Her motto was "it will be what it will be." She made the best of the days she had. I remember a day when I took her for chemotherapy. We had Zack Brown "Toes" cranked up on the CD player. She loved that CD. She said it made her think of the beach. Her happy place. It mentally put her in a good place. She'd think about the sand, water, and sun. Her daughters joined her under the umbrella. She carried that vision with her as she walked into the treatment center. It made it easier to face what would be.

You're not alone in your journey. Don't forget others when you are visioning your future. Your real joy and happiness in life will come when you begin looking for ways you can serve others. It wasn't until I started working with sorority women this really hit home. I'd always volunteered and helped out in the community, but I did it more out of a sense of responsibility. When I began working with the women and allowing their stories and struggles to become a part of my world, it made a huge difference in my thinking.

I looked for ways I could share my journey to help them reach theirs. Sometimes that was sitting and listening. At other times, it meant helping them planning a course that helped them reach their desired outcome in school get on a career path. When your vision includes others, you don't only get the pretty parts. Opening up and giving myself meant I shared real events in these women's lives. I've witnessed these women survive things that would make most want to pack up, go home, pull the covers over their heads, and say *no more*. We've struggled through the death of parents and siblings, cried over the loss of a family home, helped heal following date rape, secured financial aid, and many other trials and tribulations. What I learned is that we draw strength from each other and it's our job to grab hold and give each other that arm up when we can.

Your vision enlarges to encompass the people who matter. It becomes more when you look outside your needs and focus on helping others who are struggling meet theirs.

Want a deeper edit? *1. Grow your vision. Close your eyes and picture yourself doing what you love. Describe what you see. 2. Set clear deadlines and goals for yourself that will allow you to make that vision a reality. 3. Who shares your vision? Find like-minded people who will encourage and help you as you write the next chapter of your life.*

...5...

Embrace the Art of Surrender

The moment when you realize you need to ask for help may
be the most freeing moment you feel. It's not giving up.

DON'T FREAK OUT. I'm not telling you to throw in the towel
and be a doormat. Surrender is the fine art of letting go.

At some point, we all must acknowledge we need help from
someone else. We must give up a little control to accomplish our
big plan. The moment when you realize you need to ask for help
may be the most freeing (and frightening) moment you feel. It's
not giving up. It doesn't make you weak.

Humans are incredibly prideful. That's why it's so challenging to realize we need to rely on others at times. We must learn
to let go and to accept the help.

Successful women learn you can't do it all, all of the time. A
great leader is one who can recognize and utilize the strengths of
those around them.

Think of it like physical therapy. If you're injured, no one
expects you to jump right back out on the playing field until
you are fully healed. A therapist gives you the right exercise,

encouragement, and motivation to regain your top performance speed once again. It's the same for you when you ask for help. It's not saying you won't reach the finish line. It's asking—can you help me get there?

We've all had situations in life that bring us to our knees. You started a business, and it went belly up. You found true love, only to learn it was a one-sided commitment. We love control, and it's hard for us to accept there are things in life we cannot control no matter what we do. We fight it. We exhaust ourselves. It's painful. Then the realization hits that it's time to give in.

That's when I turn to God and say, "I can't fix it. I can't change it. It hurts. Get me through to the other side." Prayer becomes my ally and strength. When we do that, there's almost an immediate peace that accompanies the decision. We're not giving up on the problem, only on the idea that we can fix it alone. It's like giving yourself permission to grab the life preserver in front of you and hang on until the rescue boat arrives.

Surrendering does not take your power away. It's courageous. It allows you to tap into the strength of others. Trusting others can leave us fearful and vulnerable, but you must trust the process. It's not easy, but it could be the best decision you make.

Want a deeper edit? 1. *What area do you need to surrender? What burden are you carrying alone you cannot fix? 2. What would happen if you let everything remain as it is? Quit trying to fix it? 3. What are you so attached to that you weren't sure you could let go?*

move
—
moov/

verb

1. go in a specified direction or manner; change position.
"she stood up and moved to the door"
synonyms: go, walk, proceed, progress, advance;

2. change or cause to change from one state, opinion, sphere, or activity to another.
"the school moved over to the new course in 1987"
synonyms: change, budge, shift one's ground, change one's tune, change one's mind, have second thoughts;

noun

1. a change of place, position, or state.
"she made a sudden move toward me"
synonyms: movement, motion, action

When we write, there are times we need to reorder our thoughts so they make sense. There are also times in our life that a move is what we need either professionally or personally. It could be a career change. It could be stepping back from a relationship. It can be learning how to manage our expectations and emotions, shift things around, and to enable ourselves to enjoy the things and people in our lives that matter.

... | ...

Move the Clock

Step with care and great tact for life is a great balancing act.
—Dr. Suess

WE CAN WORK hard, make a good living, and complete projects, but one thing we can't do is add more hours to the day.

Regardless of what type of business you are in, our days are comprised of thinking, speaking, and acting. There are some factors we can't totally control during the day. This could be interruptions due to phone calls, questions from customers, and co-workers who need information. You could walk in from lunch and find the dreaded blue screen of death on your PC. A team member could be out sick. Your boss might come in with a priority project that wasn't on your schedule.

While there are some things you can't control, there are many factors within our control. A great tip is put a sign on your door that lets people know you can't be disturbed from x time to y time. If you don't feel you can be that bold, try this. Make a sign that says, "on a conference call" and tape it to your office door. I've used this one many times. No one has even knocked when that was stuck to the door. This small trick will limit the distractions from people who simply want to stop in and see how your day is going.

You must plan. Start the day with a priority list. Try not to jump from project to project. Limit your distractions caused by email or web surfing. Pick designated times during the day to check messages and respond. Turn off your notifications off so you aren't compelled to look every time a new message comes in. One of my best tips is to touch an email only once. You can delete it. You can set it aside to respond later if you need follow-up information or time to think about your response. You can save it for reference later or respond to it immediately. Don't open and close them over and over throughout the day.

Procrastination is a big problem. All of us are tempted at times to put off something we don't really enjoy or want to do. Admit it, multitasking is bad! You can't really concentrate on more than one thing at a time and do it well.

There're a few ways you can tackle the scheduling nightmare and free up pockets of time you need, whether it's for small projects or you need to give yourself time to work on life goals.

1. Make sure you are setting goals. Give them deadlines, and identify all the steps you think need to be in place to successfully complete your mission. Once you have the list of goals, you need to prioritize them.

2. When you start prioritizing them, make sure you list them from most important to least important, not based on which you will enjoy working on most. Handle things once. Someone once told me to either do it, delegate it, or dump it. That is terrific advice.

3. Quit procrastinating. If you find yourself saying, "I'll do it later." Stop. Break the difficult tasks up into manageable chunks. Establish time slots to deal with each slot. Put harder tasks in the time blocks where you are most productive. Learn your procrastination signals. Does the world wide web call your name? Can you ignore email

notifications? Do you check Facebook or Instagram every 15 minutes? (Is so, go back and reread the "Deleting Distraction" section.) Are there times of the day you are more productive than others? Learn to avoid the triggers that derail your progress. Reward yourself along the way. Get your favorite coffee. Treat yourself to a nice lunch out of the office instead of eating in. Remember we need more celebrations in our life!

4. Scheduling is important. Leave gaps in your schedule for things that pop up in the day. Use one calendar for work, family, and personal appointments. This way you don't overlook or cross book your day. If you hold meetings, adhere to a time schedule. Others will respect the fact you respect their time as well. Stick to a start and stop time.

5. Finally, take the last 30 minutes of your day to plan for the next day. That way you'll come in with a plan in place and be ready to tackle what's in front of you.

Where do our 24 hours go?

Think about it. We try to spend about eight hours a day sleeping. But who gets that? I'm lucky to get about five hours a night. We spend about an hour a day on personal care (some of us more). Typically, we spend about eight and a half hours at work. Then, there is the time we spend taking care of family, chores, and the house. This accounts for another five hours each day. That's at least 22 hours.

Let's be real. We can't give up work, sleep, or family. So, what are you going to give up to find more time for a project or personal passion that requires some of the time that's already allotted?

Think about it this way. What if you could gain 12 extra minutes every workday?

12 more minutes x 5 work days = 1 extra hour per week or 52 hours a year

What would you do with that time?

Successful women learn how to not only manage their time professionally but to do the same thing in their private life too.

We all have that time of day where we are at our peak. You might be a night owl, or maybe you enjoy the time of day where the sun is just starting to lighten the sky (Ugh, I can't believe there are really those of you out there!). Pick your peak to do the things that need your highest level of energy. If that's when your creative juices start flowing, then use that to your advantage. Washing clothes and straightening the den can wait until later. Oh, and put out your "do not disturb" sign too. Let your family and friends know this is your time. They will learn to respect that if you make it a priority.

On the flip side, you've got to know when to quit. Spending hours of your time on something that doesn't bring you joy is a waste, and it sucks the enjoyment right out of your life. Those tasks don't have to be perfect. Get them done and move on.

Each day, ask yourself "what's important to me and what is the best use of my time?" Mindfulness matters. Think through all the things that monopolize your time.

Be selective about the people you allow to make demands on your time. This will allow you more time to say yes to the projects, volunteer opportunities, and family activities that really matter to you. Saying no isn't bad. It's very respectful in some ways. It's better to say no to some activities you know you won't give your all to, then to show up only half interested and willing to only make a go of things. Make sure what and who you choose to invest in are quality uses of your time.

Track it. Make a list. Cross off items. I've even been known to put items on my list that I'm already finished with or know I'll finish easily so I can have the joy of marking them off. Don't laugh, I know some of you do the same thing. We can't help needing that feeling of accomplishment. When we can mark it off and know we've got something done, it's a great feeling.

Finally, invest in some quiet time. I know meditation is all the buzz. I'm not a sit still and quiet kind of girl. I do my best thinking when I'm in the tub or traveling in the car. Crank up the music and let the thoughts flow. I use that time to think through project ideas, dissect people issues, or simply shut out people and problems for a while. It's my talk to God time. I don't think of it as prayer as much as I like to have conversations with him. Don't neglect your spirituality, and don't think your time must follow some pattern laid out in a book or Sunday School lesson from someone else.

Learn to ask yourself a simple question all throughout the day – "Is this what I need to be doing right now or is it what I want to be doing?"

Managing time isn't about finding more hours in the day; it's about using the ones you do have to the best of your ability.

Want a deeper edit? 1. Identify what your most productive time of day is and make a plan to use that to your advantage when you schedule meetings, projects, or other items that require concentration or energy. 2. This week, first thing in the morning make a to-do list based on priorities (most important to complete today at the top on down to the least). Start with the top item and don't move to the next until you can mark it off as complete. Then at the end of the day, go ahead and move the items you didn't complete over to the next along with anything new for that day. When you come in the next morning, you'll be ready to start the day. 3. What would you do with one extra hour per week?

...2...

Move Through the Dark or Difficult Times

What you've experienced and lived through helps you be more compassionate and gives you the insight to help others.

AS MUCH AS we hate talking about it, there will be times in life where we all face trials. It could be the death of a close friend or family member, a divorce, or even a health scare. So how do you continue to work and lead others amid your own personal crisis? Can you still show up authentically for others when you are merely trying to get through the day?

We all like to put on that perfect face for others, but remember it is your humanity and life experience that makes you strong. What you've experienced and lived through helps you be more compassionate and gives you the insight to help others.

Being perfect isn't what makes you a good leader or a good friend. Your ability to keep going in the face of adversity is. Be kind to yourself. Don't expect more of yourself than you would of someone else. Give yourself permission to grieve or be mad. Acknowledging your own journey allows you to relate to what is going on in the life of someone else.

Life happens, and it's not always pretty. Things we haven't planned on upset our normally-ordered days. Don't fall into the *the world is conspiring and it's out to get me* thought process. There will be things that come along you can't control.

In 1995, Susan M. showed me this strength. I interviewed her for a breast cancer awareness section that ran in the lifestyle section of the local daily newspaper.

"I found the lump myself while I was on a trip to Charleston with my daughter," she said. "I didn't say anything to her about it. I went to the doctor immediately when I returned home. I went to the OB/GYN one day and then straight to the surgeon. I had a biopsy, and it came back positive."

She chose a mastectomy with continued drug treatment. Prayer and family helped Susan get through. "After realizing what I'd had done, I turned it over to God. I decided whatever happened, happened."

Susan attributed attitude with a crucial role in her recovery process.

"I decided right away that I was going to get up from surgery and get on with my life. I went to England three weeks after my surgery. I had made the plans long before the surgery, and I didn't see the need to change them."

Even making a choice to face cancer head-on, one of the first emotions Susan felt was fear.

"It's never far from your mind," she said. "Any ache or pain you have, you think it's back. You just can't think it's going to stop you from doing everything you have always wanted to do. The fear is always there. I get scared every time I go back for a checkup and mammogram. You learn to accept it and go on with your life."

Fear is natural, she said.

"You can't help but feel a little afraid when you are faced with the kind of choices you are going to have to make."

Your support network is vital.

"My family and friends were a great comfort to me," she said. "My family didn't baby me, so I got right back up and got right back into life. My friends have been by my side through the whole process."

Susan continued to have an optimistic outlook throughout her journey.

"It makes you appreciate every day. The small things you might have worried about before, just don't seem as important as they once did."

We all face battles, but the key is determining how we overcome.

We must identify the enemy. Maybe our own attitude hinders us and keeps us from moving forward. Perhaps it's issues in our marriage. You can't move past something until you shed light on it.

Ask for help. We can't solve every problem alone. Don't assume someone else knows what you are dealing with. Instead of drowning in issues, ask for a life preserver.

Talk to God. I mean have real conversations. I've yelled, cried, laughed, and shared about every emotion possible in my talks with God. A lot of them happen in the shower or in the car. It's my alone time.

Don't let yourself drift off course. Don't forget your values as a way to cover up the feelings you hold inside. That's why it's so important not to keep them bottled up inside.

Celebrate a small victory every day. You woke up. You got out of bed. You decided to face the day when you only wanted to pull the covers back over your head, roll over, and sleep until next month.

Remember you aren't alone. You've got friends and family that have your back, and they will be a source of strength for you. While you may keep that part of your life private in the workplace, you don't have to keep it from that core group of people in your life. Having that outlet is a good thing.

Discouragement is a deadly disease. It happens when we are run down, not sleeping, and frustrated with what life is dishing out. You must fight that gloomy outlook. Put your galoshes on and go stomp in the puddles. Don't give up hope.

As crazy as it sounds, have conversations out loud with yourself. Science shows talking out loud to yourself moves you forward and combats negativity. When the alarm goes off, sit up and tell the world, "I'm getting out of bed today." Then get up and get dressed. Next, "I can make it through today." No "I don't" or "I can't" allowed in these conversations. Remember to be kind to yourself. If you are experiencing a rough patch, think about what you'd say to comfort a friend. Now turn around and say it out loud to yourself. Be convincing. Use your name in the sentence. Tell yourself that you've got this.

Give yourself permission to enjoy people throughout the day. Find joy where it surfaces. If you can muster the energy to celebrate the accomplishment of others, you'll be surprised at how that feeling of happiness will carry with you for hours after you leave their presence. You can let your troubles go for a little while and experience a temporary release.

Give yourself permission to take a personal day. If you need it, take a day and stay in bed binge-watching comedies on your favorite streaming service You may need a day to sleep and rebuild your energy. Emotions can cause physical effects. They are draining. Know yourself well enough to know when you need that moment to recharge. You can't lead people if you allow yourself to get depleted.

We always say distractions are a bad thing. In this case, they can be a blessing. Our brains can't pay attention to everything at once. Distractions can help lessen the pain you are going through. Playing games that require thinking can help redirect your brain from focusing on a loss. Words with Friends, anyone?

No one expects you to be a superhero every day. We're all human. It's our humanity that makes us great friends and co-workers. Take care of you, and you'll be able to take care of those in your charge.

Want a deeper edit? 1. *Think about a dark or difficult time you've experienced. What lessons did you learn?* 2. *Did you allow anyone to see your vulnerability and hurt? Why, or why not?* 3. *How can you grow from this experience and use it in the future? How does it help you lead others?*

••• 3 •••

Move past failure

Your success is determined by how fast you pick yourself up,
dust off, and jump back into the next project.

THOMAS EDISON SAID, "I haven't failed. I've just found 10,000 ways that wouldn't work". J.K. Rowling was on welfare when she wrote *Harry Potter and the Sorcerer's Stone* and had the manuscript rejected by 12 publishers. Stephen King's first book, *Carrie*, was rejected 30 times, which prompted him to throw it in the trash. His wife retrieved it and encouraged him to send it to another publisher. Walt Disney's first animation company went bankrupt. Failure hits everyone; it doesn't discriminate.

It's important to look at how fast you bounce back when something goes wrong. How long does it take for you to get back up when failure knocks you flat on your butt?

So, you got shot down by your boss. A campaign you spent months on doesn't generate the numbers you expected. Whatever the cause, failure is going to happen to everyone at some point.

Why does failure stick with us longer than success? We tend to focus on the negative. Humans are hardwired to do that. It goes all the way back to cavemen times when people had to anticipate hard times and plan to survive.

Your success is determined by how fast you pick yourself up, dust off, and jump back into the next project. Unsuccessful people wallow. They beat themselves up. They sit back on the couch and watch marathons of Netflix shows while their creative energy leaks out between the cushions. Instead of dissecting the problem, they let their self-doubt, fears, and judgment keep them from moving forward.

Holding on to regret is like carrying a backpack loaded down with hundreds of pounds everywhere you go, 24 hours a day. It's draining. It stops you from participating in life.

The great news is you can learn to speed up the recovery. In three easy steps, you can turn on the burn and get ready to get back into the game.

1. Forgive yourself. No really. Use nice talk when you think about your role and the project. If you wouldn't talk to a co-worker that way, then don't talk to yourself that way.

2. Examine what went wrong. Don't let emotions cloud your analysis of the project. Learn from your mistakes and find ways to prevent the same thing from happening on the next project.

3. Move on. The best way to get over it is to dive into another project (and if your desk is like mine, you're sure to have one waiting). You know the old saying—get back on the horse that bucks you off. The feeling of successfully pulling a project together will make the sting of a past failure fade into the mist.

Don't get stuck looking in the rearview mirror. If that becomes your vision, you'll never move past it. Work to see the bright side. Use self-talk. Rehearse talking about the good things or lessons you've learned. Rehashing the bad only amplifies its impact on your mind.

Want a deeper edit? 1. Why do we allow failure to stick with us longer than our successes? 2. Think of a failure you have experienced. How did you handle it? What could you have done to bounce back and move forward? 3. Is there a failure currently holding you back? Examine what went wrong, forgive yourself, and move forward.

...4...

Move the Conversation

We must get back to a place where we can have real discussions without fear. Simply because opinions and ideas are different, doesn't mean they are threatening.

WE NEED MORE real conversations. I mean the kind where people on opposite sides of the fence sit down and really talk about ideas, opinions, and viewpoints.

Civility and the ability to have a frank, open conversation is becoming a lost art. Sharing opposing viewpoints while remaining polite and courteous is hardly seen. Is it so hard to maintain respectful behavior while dialoguing in a heated debate?

If you watch the news, look around our communities, or spend any time on social media, you know it's becoming harder and harder to find what a conversation like this would look like. Nasty comments left anonymously have become the norm on social posts. People are empowered thanks to the fact they no longer have to take ownership of statements. It emboldens people to say things in a much sharper manner than they might if they were having the conversation face to face with someone.

Even more alarming is what I see in day-to-day life. People seem to have no regard for the feelings of others. Simply listen to the daily exchanges in line at any fast food restaurant or while you are grocery shopping, and you're likely to witness an exchange that should make you a little uncomfortable.

It seems we allow emotions to take over much more quickly now. Comments are taken as personal attacks. We no longer allow comments to roll off our backs, shake our head, and think *bless their little heart—their ignorance is showing.*

People have no fear of any consequences that come from sharing their comments, despite the fact people have lost their jobs after some of these encounters have been videoed and circulated around the internet.

It seems the worse the behavior is, the more people are fascinated by it. It should cause you to recoil, but instead, people share it and give it more traction.

This is spreading into all areas of life, and it's becoming harder and harder for people to have conversations concerning politics, religion, community needs, and more. There seems to be less and less listening or discussion and more reactions.

Civility is working at staying present even when the people around you are passionate about and have deep-seated beliefs which fall out on the other side of the fence from you.

We've got to find places and ways to disagree without being disagreeable. We can't ignore what we don't agree with. It doesn't merely go away.

We must get back to a place where we can have real discussions without fear. Simply because opinions and ideas are different doesn't mean they are threatening. Without a real exchange of ideas, there is no real chance to grow or share opposing viewpoints. You can't learn if you only listen to one point of view.

That's what I love about my group of friends. We have such diverse backgrounds and beliefs that conversation is always lively. We can talk politics and religion. We can talk about current events. We can disagree and argue our points. At the end of the evening, no one may have shifted their views, but we all still hug and can't wait until the next time we're together.

We grow stronger, not weaker when we engage with others and ideas we disagree with. It's important to talk to find common ground. That common ground allows us to build, and to really begin having the chance to make real change in communities, the workplace, and even in our own homes.

__Want a deeper edit?__ 1. What topics would you like to have a real discussion about to earn a better understanding? 2. Based on your topics, who are the people you need to invite for conversation and idea sharing? 3. How can you control your emotional triggers to engage in tough conversations? How are you prepared to listen and not react?

...5...

Move Your Career Forward

Make sure you are marketing yourself smartly.

NO MATTER IF you're only starting out in your career or you've been working the same job for years, you've got the power to move your career in a new direction. If you've already got your eye on that next rung up the ladder, let's talk about what you can do to get ahead.

If you want to stay with the same company, you need to make yourself stand out from everyone else. There are 10 things you can do that will help you rise in the ranks.

1. Be positive. No one likes a negative Nancy. People notice your attitude.

2. Make sure your boss isn't surprised. If you know something is brewing (internally or externally) make sure it's not anything that is going to take your boss by surprise.

3. Don't bring problems to your boss. Bring solutions. Don't like how something is going? Don't go complain. Come up with a plan and present it.

4. Do your homework. Know what's going on in the company and the industry. It's important that you keep up with trends, changes, and challenges your industry faces.

5. Keep perspective. Is what you are doing in line with the plans of the company? Does it move things forward? Ask to see the strategic plan. Work with your supervisor on ways to align your skills with those the company needs to move ahead. Your drive and willingness to learn will not go unnoticed.

6. Stay focused. What is the company mission? How are you helping achieve it? When you are away from the desk and out in the community do you further that mission? Are you sitting at a little league game in a logoed shirt badmouthing your boss? You'd be surprised how fast these conversations make it back to the office.

7. Use active listening. I've always heard that you have two ears and one mouth. Listen twice as long as you talk. Let someone finish their thought before you jump in with a comment.

8. Nurture your reputation. Look the part. Be known as a problem solver. Work with integrity. Make sure the work you complete is correct.

9. Learn a new trick. Each year add a new skill to your basket. It adds value to you and to the company.

10. Know what your boss sees as a priority. Help her/him accomplish what matters to them. Make an appointment to talk to the person above you or even the CEO. Most people never want to have conversations with these people unless there is a problem. Show your genuine interest, and you'll make a big impression. Ask them to help you

develop a plan that will aid your professional advancement. Most supervisors and CEOs like when employees take the initiative.

If you are willing to look outside your current organization, consider all your skills. Analyze every aspect of the job you currently do and those you've had in the past. Make sure you have a current list of all skills and certifications you can use to advance. Keep your resume current with any courses, awards, or activities that add to your employability.

Use the Internet for research. There are so many job sites; search through the listings and see where your unique skill set might apply. Don't get stuck on a job title. If there is a particular job you are interested in but lack a few essential skills, make a plan to acquire them. You can even mention in an interview you've invested in you by adding to your skills.

Be careful you don't earn the reputation of being a job hopper. Make sure you stick around long enough to acquire skills and knowledge. People in charge of hiring do pay attention to the length of stay.

Make sure you are marketing yourself smartly. Blog about industry-related topics. Use social media channels to show off your skills and abilities effectively. Speaking of social media, clean it up if you are seriously job hunting, especially if your account is public. Most hiring professionals check out your social profile before they even bring you in for an initial interview. Don't let a few bad posts keep you from getting that interview you are counting on.

Find a mentor in the field you aspire to work in. They can be a great resource not only for learning about openings in your area of interest, but they can make introductions and recommendations for you as well. Building this network won't only benefit you in the job search but will continue to be an asset once you've received your dream position.

Every job requires some form of communication. Spend time on this skill. It goes without saying you should be friendly and professional in your written or spoken interactions. There are numerous groups where you can get experience in this area. Invest that time, and you're sure to see dividends.

Most importantly, don't show up at an interview—even an internal one—unprepared. Show that you've put the work in learning the industry and you're ready to use your skills to be a problem solver and team player.

The search for your dream job may be a long and tedious process. Don't get discouraged. Continue to focus on the next step. Stay positive. Cultivate relationships. Do all this, and you'll have that job offer sooner than you think.

> ***Want a deeper edit?*** *1. Describe your dream job. Skills you need? Duties? Location? Environment? Culture? 2. Identify your skills that line up with this job. What areas do you need to increase your education? 3. Identify trends in the industry you want to work in. Where is growth occurring? What are the current threats? How can you prepare for each?*

···6···

Propel Yourself Forward

Find the inspiration you need to do the things you enjoy.
This push will fuel you with determination to meet all
life's craziness head-on and with purpose.

DO YOU FEEL like juggling your commitments to work, family, friends, church, and even your pet leave you shaking your head at the end of the day? There are days where I'd like to flip off the adult switch and stay on the couch under a warm blanket. I want to yell, "I don't feel like adulting today!"

Working a full-time job, taking care of those who matter, and still carving out the time you need to be creative can be a challenge. So many of us worry if we take that *me time* people will think we aren't giving our all, or that we are wasting our time on something that doesn't matter. Everything we do well is driven by a passion and a desire to do whatever it takes to produce the best results. For some of us, that means it's time to embrace the imperfect and messy. For others, it means saying no to something that doesn't give you that lift or keeps you from spending time developing a talent or skill you enjoy.

When you reach that point, it's time to *PROPEL*.

P—Push yourself. Do something out of your comfort zone. Grow your skills. Increase your circle of acquaintances and friends. Join new groups. Find the inspiration you need to do the things you enjoy. This push will fuel you with determination to meet all life's craziness head-on and with purpose.

R—Rejoice in life's blessings. Take a moment to be thankful each day. Let it be a reminder of how far you've come and all you can to look forward to. An attitude of gratitude will leave you feeling ready for tomorrow.

O—Organize. Use a planner. Don't let all the little things sneak up on you. Put everything on your calendar. If you don't know about an appointment or a school program, you can't account for it. These unscheduled interruptions in your day can steal precious moments. They throw deadlines off. They keep you from meeting goals. Of course, there are still things that will crop up unexpectedly. The kids will get sick. The pipe bursts. But 90% of the time, the chaos in our schedules come because we didn't plan.

P-Prioritize our choices. When you split your energy between too many things, you end up feeling lost and unaccomplished. Spend time each day (or week) and make a priority list. Then, use it to make sure you give the items that matter the care and attention they deserve.

E- Energize yourself so that you are ready to face another day. Our passion and drive is our energy source. While our time may be limited, our inner fire isn't. You've got to take the time to focus it so that all areas of your life get fueled. It may be time to connect with your spirituality; write the words that are running through your mind or playing a rowdy game of corn hole in the backyard with your kids. Whatever it takes to refuel your tank, make that a priority.

L-Learn to experience *new* every day. Explore new things, writers, music, places, and food when you have the opportunity. Broaden your view.

By propelling yourself forward year after year, you'll ensure you genuinely show up and give the right amount of attention and focus to the things that matter. It will provide you with the balance you need and take you to new levels.

> ***Want a deeper edit?*** *1. What is the one thing outside your comfort area you'll attempt to try? 2. How will you organize your week to allow time for you to reach your goal? 3. For one month, try one new thing each week. It might be a new type of food, listening to a different genre of music, or maybe it's trying your hand at painting with watercolors. Document your journey and how you feel along the way.*

$\bullet \bullet \bullet 7 \bullet \bullet \bullet$

Pay it Forward

Teachers aren't the only ones who can impact the direction someone takes in life. Each of us has that ability.

ONE OF THE best things you can do is find a mentor and in return, be a mentor.

While working as the feature's editor for a local, daily newspaper, I had the privilege of interviewing Alice Thornton. At the time she was 92 ½ years old and a community icon who touched thousands of lives each year by bringing history to life at the Pike Pioneer Museum. Had it not been for a teacher early on, the community might have missed out on her special gift. She was a spinner and a weaver. She not only wove cloth, but she showed me how to adapt when changes occur and still weave our passions into our life.

Her inspiration for weaving came from her husband Van.

"We had both been appointed to teach at the central college in Oklahoma around 1930," she said. "He taught industrial arts at the college. Back then, they lumped industrial art and design in with the art department. We kind of got thrown together. His wife had died, and after about one month of teaching together, we realized we enjoyed each other's company. Then two years later, we married. Back then there was a law that said, 'no two people in the family could hold a job,' so I quit my teaching job at the college, stayed home, and tended the house."

Her husband attended a national industrial arts meeting, and it was there he decided she needed to try weaving.

"He watched a demonstration on weaving," she said. "He came home all excited about it. He made me my own loom in his shop. When he finished, he put all the parts in a bundle. It was still in the bundle when he died of cancer in 1945. I didn't really know what the loom was until some men from the university put it together for me. When he died, I applied at John Brown University in Arkansas and got the job in the art department. It was there I really learned to weave."

Alice said she started teaching that fall, and because the school was in the Ozark Mountains, they offered nine semester hours of weaving. She said she knew how excited her husband was about the loom and when the opportunity to learn presented itself, she took it.

"The mountain people handed down the skill and knowledge from generation to generation. They started a weaver's guild, and the college began an art instruction course on it. The college allowed me, as a teacher, to take the class in between my required ones."

Her husband might have opened her eyes to the love of spinning and weaving, but it was a fifth-grade teacher who started her down her path.

"It was then I was placed in a class with an art teacher who helped me develop my talents," she said. "She recognized my skill in those early activities. I am very headstrong and believe people today don't develop the creative side of themselves as they should. They don't have people showing them how to any longer. Most people think of what I do as play. But it's not. It takes a great deal of skill to do these things, more so than reading a book. Later, I went on to teach teachers how to develop those skills in their students. I found my calling at an early age. I had good sensitive teachers who helped me find the way. Teachers today need to be the same way. Every child is not made the same. They have different abilities. If we could only find those abilities in each child, there would not be so many of the bad things we have now. Those children just have no way of expressing themselves in a positive manner."

Her husband's death left the artist in need of a job that would allow her to support their four children plus two stepchildren from her husband's previous marriage. She was in a low-paying teaching position at a small evangelical college at the time.

"I attended a national education meeting held in St. Louis," she said. "I was keeping my ear out for a new job, and I found one. Over the loudspeaker came an announcement saying there was an opening for a woman with a master's degree in art at Troy State University. So, I met with Dr. Gracie and was hired. I had never been south of Oklahoma before I moved (to Troy, AL) in 1953 with the children. I had to learn a new way of living and adapt to a new place, but I think we did well for ourselves."

Alice went on to teach art education at Troy University for 18 years. She retired and found her old love of weaving would now fill the time she had once devoted to teaching. In 1971, she went to work for the museum helping them get ready to open to the public. As the resident weaver, her demonstrations kept an artform alive for thousands of visitors.

Teachers aren't the only ones who can impact the direction someone takes in life. Each of us has that ability. People tend to think of mentors as coming from their same occupational set. It's great to have one there, but why limit yourself. Mentors can help you in all areas of life—spiritually, creatively, and professionally.

To make the most of that relationship, you've got to pick the right person first. I suggest you come up with a set of goals and ideas you can share with that person during your initial meeting. It's important that you both have a clear idea of the expectations and outcomes you are seeking.

Make sure the person has time for you or you have time to devote to another person. Mentor/mentee relationships require an investment of time. If either of you is not going to commit to the process, it won't be fruitful.

These relationships need to be open and honest. Part of the expectation is not only sharing successes, but also failures. These discussions can help you grow. Are you both comfortable in being a little vulnerable?

Do they seem to be enthusiastic about the process? You need someone who is excited to share the journey with you. Someone who is willing to answer questions and share your journey. They need to be a resource and help you set goals that will lead you closer to your ultimate path.

If you are the mentee, you owe them a few things in the relationship as well. You need to be on time for your meetings. You need to be fully engaged in the process. That means not checking your phone every five minutes. It means you are willing to put their advice into action. Set a schedule for your meetings and keep them. Make sure you talk upfront about how much and how often you will contact them. Is it ok to text, call, or email if something comes up? Are there hours of the day they don't want to be bothered? Remember, in every life things come up. If they need to cancel or reschedule, it's ok.

Remember, your mentor is not there to solve your problems but to offer wisdom learned from their journey. So be prepared for a real discussion.

It's not a one-way street. Make sure you are sharing with your mentor too. You have skills or talents that would be helpful to them. If you ran across the best article that relates to their field, send it to them. Don't be afraid to share ideas or suggestions with them as well.

Learn about each other's lives outside of work. Share what your life is like. The more real you can be, the better you'll get along. You can also learn a lot about how to balance different areas of work and life. You might find you have a common charitable interest too.

Be prepared. When you meet, have a set of questions or a situation in mind to discuss. Having a point of focus will make your time more productive and keep you from getting lost in a sea of what ifs. Be intentional with your time and theirs.

These relationships don't have to be permanent. If it's not working or you feel like you aren't connecting, it's ok to move on. Thank them for their time and willingness to share with you. I'd suggest you consider a short-term arrangement, in the beginning, to see how things go. Try it for three months. If it seems to be working and you both agree to continue, then that's awesome. However, if it's not, you have a built-in out with no hurt feelings.

On a final note, don't feel like you must settle for one mentor. Your path will take many turns, and there are a lot of people with a wealth of information to share. Take advantage of that. Hopefully, if your mentor works in a field you are considering, they will introduce you to other people too. You might find people who interest you in many areas who are willing to share what they have learned along the way.

Want a deeper edit? *1. Have you had a successful mentor/mentee relationship? What made it work? If it didn't, what caused the failure? 2. What gift, talent, or skill can you share with someone else? 3. In what areas of your life (personal or professional) would a mentor be helpful? Are there people you automatically think of who would fill that role? If not, where can you look?*

···8···

Move Through the Open Door

I'm a firm believer that doors open for a reason, and they open at the right time.

IF YOU THINK about it, our lives are like a series of rooms. Each door we walk through takes us to a new place. We walk through one the first day we leave the comfort of home and walk into a kindergarten class. From there, it's one twist of a knob after another.

I'm a firm believer that doors open for a reason, and they open at the right time. (They close too, but that's for another time.)

It wasn't too long ago that I walked through one that opened for me.

After working for 20 years in a job I'd have told you I would retire from, I gave the knob of opportunity a huge twist and pushed the door wide open. I resigned, took on a new role, packed up, moved across state lines, and left the comfort of family and friends miles behind.

Every action has a catalyst. Mine came in the form of a single email. It put this whole journey in motion. I'd had a particularly bad week at work with a new manager (ok more like a horrible six months). I reached my breaking point while working an event on a Friday night when most people were already at home with their families for the weekend. My inbox dinged signaling the arrival of an email from my manager. In it, he basically implied my journalism degree came from a box of cereal, that my writing wasn't personal enough, and his child, a math major, knew more about putting together a magazine than I did. This came from the same guy who didn't think it was important enough to sit and talk about what he'd like to say to our customers. I was told to "Make it up. That's what you're good at, right?"

Something about this email pushed me over the edge. I remember fighting back emotion and turning my phone off so that I didn't respond with all the things flying around in my head. (That goes back to knowing your hot buttons and how to deal with them. I'd have been fired if I had replied with what went through my mind.) A colleague from another company was sitting across from me and asked if everything was ok. This only made the moment worse.

I'm as transparent as they come. You can look at my face and know what I'm thinking. I'd make a crappy poker player. I sat there through the dinner and the words cemented themselves in my heart. I felt empty and tired. I cried all the way home. It wasn't because my feelings were hurt; it was because I felt totally devalued.

Saturday morning, I woke up with an email from another colleague telling me about an opening in another state she thought I'd be a perfect fit for (Remember us talking about the importance of making real connections?). I read the description, filled out the application, and hit submit. I count my lucky stars her email arrived when it did.

It took a big moment for me to realize I'd become complacent and that merely good enough wasn't really good enough. It had become only going through the motions. In my heart, I knew my vision wasn't in line with the course new management took, and I also knew that my skills weren't valued. I'd feel myself physically react to pulling into the parking lot at the office. My stomach would get tight, I'd have to put on a forced smile, and make myself open the door and go in.

That's not healthy or productive. When the bad days begin to happen more frequently than the good ones, you need to seriously consider if you are where you need to be.

Don't linger at a threshold because you are afraid of leaving the comfortable behind. Don't let the what ifs hold you back. There will be voices in your head telling you to stay with what you know, you're not good enough, or they will laugh at you. I'm telling you to be brave and walk right on through with your head held high.

I'm also not telling you it's ok to give up simply because something is hard. There's a difference in a hard patch and being in a place that is sucking up your joy. We must put effort into staying passionate about our relationships and our work. There was something there initially that caused you to dream dreams. Don't let a small disappointment derail you. It's also up to us to know when there are enough embers left to reignite your passion or if the fire is truly extinguished.

Trust your inner voice. Don't let someone else's version of your life hold you back. You know what is best for you. Honor those feelings that start deep in the pit of your stomach and never fully go away no matter how hard you try to ignore them. If you listen, your inner wisdom and conviction will give you the confidence to move you to your fullest potential.

You'll know when it's the right door. I prayed a lot. I'd tell God to close my eyes to the opportunities that weren't where I needed to be (and he shut down a few). I watched as things lined up all along this journey. When it's the right door, you can almost feel a hand on your back giving you a proverbial shove through to the other side.

Each doorway prepares us for the next. Successfully navigating through will give you the courage to try the next door. Smile as you step across with a renewed confidence and joy of discovery.

Want a deeper edit? 1. What doorway are you looking for? 2. If you are hesitating at the threshold, what scares you about taking the step? What's the worst that can happen? What happens if you never give it a shot? 3. Are there opportunities continually showing up at your door that you've been afraid to accept because you are comfortable where you are now and afraid of what the unknown might hold?

$\bullet \bullet \bullet 9 \bullet \bullet \bullet$

Embrace Change

Stay positive. All change means you are learning or transforming.

IT'S INEVITABLE. IT'S a challenge. Sometimes it's welcome. Sometimes it's a pain. It's change. We all experience it, repeatedly.

Several years ago, I went through a management change. I had worked under the same manager for years. I knew what he liked. I knew the words he liked to use. I knew the aspects of our business that were important to him. Then, he retired.

My work experienced a period of uncertainty which generated a lot of turmoil in the office. It was a relatively small company with under 60 employees; however, the process of finding his replacement turned into more of an internal joke for the employees. Everyone felt it had been predetermined before the process began. People felt the decision makers in charge were only going through the motions to meet a legal requirement. There was a lot of tension among a few internal candidates who threw their names into the hat as contenders. There were more jokes about how the process was a waste of time. None of this made for a strong corporate culture people wanted to be a part of.

Ultimately, I left that office. The course and culture were not where I saw myself staying. What I learned was that you can only control your reaction to a situation.

There were specific things that helped me along this journey.

First, I found a group of people I could express my feelings with. In a work setting, this can be tricky. I'd like to think that co-workers won't use the information to get ahead of you, but that's not always the case. I was strategic in who I shared my feelings with. I also used my outside network of colleagues to have discussions with. You learn quickly you aren't the only one with doubts, concerns, or questions.

Document the situation. Sketch out what you see. I'm a visual person. Seeing it on paper helps me process and recognize the big picture. It enables me to make sense of all the pieces.

Know there is no right answer. Ask yourself the what ifs. What if they choose x for the job? What if he or she changes the whole corporate structure? What if the organization suffers financially? What if it turns out better than expected? Don't automatically assume you're getting the short end of the stick. If you look hard enough, you can find the positives.

Don't make rash decisions. Take some time to sleep on what's happening. You need to see the picture clearly before you can determine your best next step.

Most changes in life won't be ones that affect your career; however, they will have some impact on your life as you know it. Change doesn't have to be feared.

If it is a monumental change (like shifting careers, starting your own business, moving to a new state), try breaking it up into smaller steps. You'll feel more in control and better equipped to survive the process.

Stay flexible along the journey. The first path may not be the one you end up on. Be prepared for a few bumps along the road. Anticipating them will keep you from stressing when they occur.

Stay positive. All change means you are learning or trans-forming. No matter how big or small the circumstance, you will navigate through to the other side, and you'll come out wiser and stronger.

Thankfully, we've all been given the tools and talents we need to surpass any challenge. You may feel like there are people who have everything in life fall in place. I guarantee if you filled their shoes for a few months, you'd see the public image is way different than what happens at home each night. Each of us will face our own unique trials and challenges. When you are in periods of change, stop the urge to compare your circumstance with those around you. You can only live your life.

Throughout my corporate career and my personal relationships, I've realized different personality types adapt or handle change in many ways. Those left-brained individuals—my analytical, logical, organized friends—have a harder time with it than those of us who are right-brained, emotionally-oriented ones.

If you are responsible for managing change in a corporate space, in an organization, or even your family, you should remember you can't set a time limit on acceptance of change. Everyone moves toward acceptance at their own pace.

Just because the process has taken place, your communications don't end. Your job is to continue moving people toward acceptance and help them recover positively. People need to develop their own coping mechanism. Once they reach that point, you're nearing the finish line.

Encourage and be patient. Change means you have snatched someone's security blanket right off their lap. If you'll give them time and the right direction, you'll soon have everyone working on the same path once again.

Want a deeper edit? 1. What was the most stressful change event you've experienced? How did it make you feel? What caused you to feel uncertainty? What would have helped move you toward acceptance? 2. How can you help a change you are involved with be initiated in a manner that will garner quicker acceptance? 3. What are the what ifs you need to ask if you are in the middle of a change process now?

···IO···

Quit Hitting Snooze

Hitting the snooze button doesn't only happen when it comes to going to the gym. We let it seep into our relationships and into our careers.

IF YOU ARE waiting for motivation to strike, you'll still be waiting tomorrow. You've got to quit hitting the snooze button on life and get on with it.

I'm guilty. I'll admit it. I religiously watch American Ninja Warrior (1), get caught up in the athlete's stories, and feed off the emotion that comes from watching them attempt the series of obstacles. I watch Ted Talks and YouTube videos of the latest and greatest speakers. In my mind, I get all fired up to get healthy, start running again, or learn a new skill and then once the video is over, I grab my comfy blanket, curl up on the couch, and hope that feeling disappears as quickly as it appeared.

Words are magic to me. They inspire me. They evoke emotion. That's why they are so powerful. What they won't do is get me out of bed at 5:00 a.m. to go on a three-mile run or make me hit the gym.

You've got to put discipline behind them to create that repeatable movement that helps you achieve your goal. You can't merely decide it's a great thing to do. You've got to put one foot in front of the other and do it.

The problem with motivation is that it must magically appear each day if you are going to rely on it to change a behavior. We all know that isn't going to happen. For a behavior to stick, it must become a habit.

Instead, set yourself up for success. Acknowledge the real problem. Whatever the issue is—losing weight, spending time with someone important, or learning a new skill—it's not a priority to you now. Say it out loud. "I'd rather watch Netflix than write 500 words today because writing isn't a priority to me today."

That stings, doesn't it? It's about you making a decision.

I think the need for all those motivational quotes and videos that pop up in our social media feeds come from the need to cover up the doubt we feel about ourselves. Those videos don't tell you what to do two weeks in when things aren't going as planned. Real and lasting change takes place on the inside of each of us. It doesn't come from external forces. You yourself have the knowledge and skill to make it happen.

Hitting the snooze button doesn't only happen when it comes to exercise. We let it seep into our relationships and into our careers.

Do you treat your spouse or boyfriend like you did when you first started dating? Do you still ask and care about how their day was? Are you still affectionate? Do you call or text for no reason during the day simply to let them know you're thinking about them?

What about friendships? Do you make that effort to stay connected? No, I don't mean liking their most recent photo or post on Facebook. I mean really connecting? Do you call? Have real conversations? Having that real interaction is important. Small things are what it's all about. If you are taking care of those, then the big things that come along are much easier to handle.

The thing is, real success in any area only comes when you put in the work. It's never easy. There are always challenges. I hope you have real-life cheerleaders encouraging you along the path to go with a healthy dose of self-determination.

Want a deeper edit? 1. What are you sitting on the sidelines watching that you long to be a part of? 2. What steps do you need to take to move from snooze to action? 3. Are there relationships you are snoozing through? How can you wake them up and experience them to the fullest once again?

••• 11 •••

Move Toward Forgiveness

Forgiveness isn't about them at all. It's all about you. It's about not giving the power to hurt you any longer.

HOLDING ON TO hurt begins to take a toll on you. I know. I've held on to my fair share for years. It's hard for me to let go when someone has hurt me or someone I love. It's even harder for me if the person who hurt me is supposed to be someone I loved and trusted.

As a Christian, I've got the ultimate example to follow, but I still found it hard to turn those feelings loose. It took me a long time to realize that forgiveness wasn't giving the other person a pass. It's not saying you're ok with how you've been treated and pretending you're fine. I don't even think it's forgetting. I think it's about giving ourselves permission to say "yes, you're a jerk and you deserve pain and misery for what you did, but I'm not going to let you stop me from living my life," then moving forward and not letting your thoughts and feelings be tied up in them.

You can't wait for them to apologize. You may never say the words "I forgive you" out loud. That's ok. Being mad at them is fine. You can't let it fester. Letting go allows you to be able to move on and move past it. Don't add the weight of what they did to everything else you carry through life. Your friends are going to get tired of listening to you rehash how someone screwed you over and what your new plan for revenge is. Forgiveness isn't about them at all. It's all about you. It's about not giving them the power to hurt you any longer.

Being hurt by someone automatically makes you feel like you have the right to look down on them. That allows you to assess blame and yell at the top of your lungs "look what you did to me." You get to play the role of victim, but when you do, you are giving up control.

There was a period in my marriage where my husband started a business I didn't agree with. In fact, I felt like it happened behind my back to a degree after we had had an initial discussion about it. The business was a money pit. No amount of time, effort, or refurbishing was going to help it succeed.

That decision opened the door to mistrust and ultimately lead to us losing our home. I was embarrassed. I hid what was happening for as long as I could from family and friends. I felt failure. I felt doubt. I felt anger.

On the outside, I was a supportive wife. I knew he was beating himself up internally for the outcome. But on the inside, I wasn't at a point where I could feel any empathy for him. I was wrapped up in how I felt and how my life looked.

I tried to hide those feelings, even from the people I was closest with. I withdrew. Work became an outlet for me because going home meant trying to figure out what the next day held. I got to the point where I couldn't make small decisions like where to have lunch without breaking down and crying. It wasn't until I went to the doctor's office for a sinus infection that I realized I was depressed. The doc walked in and asked me how I was. I couldn't come up with an answer, only tears. He grabbed a box of tissues. He sat there until I got myself together and we talked about what was happening in life.

It's humbling to realize there are times you can't fix everything on your own (Remember the chapter on surrender, I lived it.). There's no shame in reaching out for help.

I got so wrapped up in what might happen, I couldn't enjoy the then and now. It wasn't an easy road to take. I hit a lot of detours. I realized dwelling on the hurt and hostility wasn't going to put me in a place I wanted to live. Forgiveness wasn't going to change what happened, but it was what put me on the path moving forward again.

My aha moment came when I realized I also had to make a choice to forgive myself. I was upset I had not been as involved in the process as I needed to be. I trusted others to make decisions for me. I reacted badly. I wasn't the supportive spouse I needed to be. Our ability to forgive directly relates to how we love and accept ourselves.

By choosing to forgive, you are embracing your own power to control the direction your life moves in. You're not allowing someone else's ideas or thoughts to keep you in place. You take responsibility for the choices and outcomes. You aren't the victim because of how someone else treated you.

Own what choice you made. Take responsibility. Did it impact someone else? Then, make it right. If not, that will continue to eat at you. You'll question whether you deserve good things. Are you a good person? That train of thought becomes very destructive to your inner being.

Before you can move forward, you need to look inside and determine what caused the behavior. Did your own insecurities cause you to make fun of someone else so that you'd feel better about you? Own it. Deal with it. Think more about the other person than yourself.

Take the big step and acknowledge you hurt them. Don't use qualifiers. You hurt them. Don't make excuses for why. If it's something you can fix, do it. If you are sincere, more than likely they will accept your apology. You can't force someone to give you forgiveness. It has to happen on their own schedule. They may not be at a point of acceptance yet. If not, you've made an honorable attempt to correct a wrong. Your slate is clean.

As hard as it is to forgive someone else, it's even harder to forgive ourselves. It's easy to get wrapped up in the feelings of guilt and self-criticism. These feelings can virtually paralyze us from trying new things or taking risks on new relationships. We all make mistakes in life. It's part of growing as a person. Many of our mistakes are simply a result of a choice we made without knowing we hadn't learned everything we needed to know yet.

Ask yourself, if someone you loved was holding on to the same fear or pain, would you want them to let it go and move forward? If the answer is yes, why would you want less for yourself? Forgiving yourself releases you to be able to start again.

Ultimately, what helped me was digging into the reasons. I know deep down his decisions were made from a desire to provide a fruitful and secure life for us. It wasn't a choice made to willfully hurt or disregard my feelings. He had demons in his past making him feel the need to prove himself over and over.

Give it time. Weeks, months, or years may pass before the pain fades and you can look back and not feel your chest tighten. Taking that first step is a hard choice, but the feeling you get knowing you are moving closer to your own peace and happiness is worth it.

Want a deeper edit? *1. Have you been carrying a hurt or wrong that you need to forgive? How has it affected you? 2. Are there unresolved issues you need to forgive yourself of so that you can begin the healing process? 3. Imagine someone mentioning the person or event and you no longer feeling pain. How will it feel knowing you've been able to move past a painful event?*

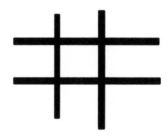

/end/
end

noun

1. a final part of something, especially a period of time, an activity, or a story.
"the end of the year"

synonyms:
conclusion, termination, ending, finish, close, resolution, climax, finale, culmination, denouement

2. the furthest or most extreme part or point of something.
"a length of wire with a hook at the end"
synonyms: extremity, furthermost part, limit

TRADITIONALLY, THIS MARK means the end of the copy. There's a lot of debate as to why and when this began appearing in newsrooms. The most commonly held belief is that "-30-" is a homage to when messages were sent across the telegraph. It denoted the end of a message in Morse code. Others claim the "-30-" comes from a time when stories were written in longhand—X marked the end of a sentence, XX the end of a paragraph, and XXX meant the end of a story. The Roman numerals XXX translate to 30. No matter which one you choose to believe, it does mark the end of my book, but not the end of your story.

From one writer to another, I hope you think of this each time you pick up your pencil.

The parable of the pencil goes something like this: (1)

There are 5 qualities of a pencil:

- It is able to do great things, but only if it allows itself to be held in someone's hand.

- It experiences a painful sharpening from time to time, but that makes it become a better pencil.

- It can correct any mistakes it might make.

- The most important part of it will always be what's inside.

- It leaves a mark on every surface it touches. No matter the condition, it must continue to write.

Now stop and think of yourself like the pencil.

- You are able to do great things, but only by allowing other people to access the many gifts and talents you possess.

- You too experience a painful sharpening from time to time. The struggles and problems in life are needed to make us stronger people.

- You have the power to correct mistakes you might make.

- The most important part of you will always be what's on the inside.

- On every surface, or person you encounter, you leave your mark. No matter what the situation, you must do your best. Always remember: you may never know the impact you have or the meaning behind a few words you share.

As you move forward, I hope you write bold words and dream big dreams, not just this year, but for each year to come. I hope you put the Life Edits into place and use them often and ruthlessly.

Delete what holds you back. Insert new ideas and experiences. Begin exploring opportunities. Move in different directions. Never lose the true, authentic self that makes you, you.

We start our life journey with our version of a fairytale. Each of us dreams of finding that successfully ever after. It's there waiting for you. You just need to write yourself as the heroine of the adventure and go for it.

Don't allow negative voices in your head or those of other people to determine the ending of your story. The next page is blank today, and it's up to you to fill it with things that bring you joy, happiness, and success. See yourself as the creator of your own story. Sharpen your pencil and write your new chapter. The book is called opportunity, and it's waiting for you to write your story.

Notes

Delete Section

Delete the Idea of Perfect

1. https://www.mayoclinic.org/healthy-lifestyle/
   stress-management/in-depth/stress-symptoms/
   art-20050987
2. https://www.webmd.com/balance/stress-management/
   effects-of-stress-on-your-body

Delete Distractions

1. https://www.telegraph.co.uk/finance/jobs/11691728/
   Employees-waste-759-hours-each-year-due-to-workp
   lace-distractions.html
2. https://www.nytimes.com/2013/05/05/opinion/sun-
   day/a-focus-on-distraction.html
3. https://stopad.io/blog/interrupted-work-statistics
4. https://www.reuters.com/article/us-work-interrup-
   tions/u-s-worker-interruptions-costly-research-s
   hows-idUSN1345262720061213

Begin Section

Be Your Best You

1. 13.1 Half Marathon Trainer from Zen Labs https://www.zenlabsfitness.com/ (https://itunes.apple.com/us/app/13-1-half-marathon-trainer/id514647091?mt=8)
2. Rock 'n' Roll Marathon Series http://www.runrockn-roll.com/
3. Dr. Kevin Elko http://www.drelko.com
4. Dr. Kevin Elko's Monday Morning Cup of Inspiration http://www.drelko.com/inspiration

Don't Let Anxiety Block Your Path

1. https://adaa.org/understanding-anxiety
2. https://www.helpguide.org/articles/anxiety/anxiety-disorders-and-anxiety-attacks.htm

Begin Connecting

1. https://en.wikipedia.org/wiki/Social_connectedness
2. http://ccare.stanford.edu/uncategorized/connectedness-health-the-science-of-social-connection-infographic/
3. https://www.socialconnectedness.org/

Insert Section

Insert Gratitude

1. https://www.psychologytoday.com/us/blog/what-mentally-strong-people-dont-do/201504/7-scientifically-proven-benefits-gratitude
2. http://time.com/5026174/health-benefits-of-gratitude/
3. https://positivepsychologyprogram.com/benefits-gratitude-research-questions/

Stet Section

Remain in Control

1. News Interviews that go wrong:
    A. https://youtu.be/hOYhkXrRAdc
    B. https://youtu.be/ALBwaO-rAsE
    C. https://youtu.be/LNbOuUpfQ2c

2. Sports Interviews gone wrong: https://www.youtube.com/watch?v=vpagwSIFEcY

Move Section

Quit Hitting Snooze

1. American Ninja Warrior: https://www.nbc.com/american-ninja-warrior

-30-

1. *The History of the Pencil – A novel by Paulo Coelho*

http://paulocoelhoblog.com/2009/12/19/the-story-of-the-pencil/

Other

Troy Messenger: https://www.troymessenger.com/
Pike Pioneer Museum: https://www.pioneer-museum.org/
Alpha Delta Pi: https://www.alphadeltapi.org/
Pancreatic Cancer Action Network: https://www.pancan.org/
National Pancreatic Cancer Foundation: https://www.npcf.us/
American Cancer Society: https://www.cancer.org/

About the Author

Chellie W. Phillips is a sweet-tea-sipping, sassy Southerner who is passionate about helping dynamic and driven women write their own success stories, find clarity, and remain true to their authentic self.

For over 20 years, she has worked in the field of public relations, marketing, and communications. Before that, she was a features editor at a daily newspaper and even dabbled in radio news. She's a speaker, motivator and a "kick-in-the-pants."

Her speaking engagements include several national and state organizations: The National Rural Electric Association of Cooperatives (NRECA)- Connect Conference, the Indiana Association of Electric Cooperatives, the Cooperative Communications Association (CCA), Co-opportunity Youth Leadership Conference, and Alpha Delta Pi Sorority.

She has served on numerous boards including NRECA Certified Cooperative Communicators, Cooperative Communicators Association, and the Newnan-Coweta Communities in School.

Her work has been recognized by the Spotlight on Excellence Program, the Cooperative Communicators Association, the Alabama Public Relations Society, and the Alabama Rural Electric Association. She received the prestigious Outstanding

Alumnus Award from the Troy University Journalism and Print Department in 2000 and the Michael Graznak Award from CCA in 2002. She was recognized by the Alabama Rural Electric Association of Cooperative in 2005 and 2007 as the Communicator of the Year.

Do you feel like you're just going through the motions at work and home? Struggling to find a balance?

Does that small voice inside encourage you to do more with your life?

You're not alone.

You have the power to change your story today!

I'm inviting you to join our community of women as we take a 6-week journey to unlock the dreams, passion, and purpose you've lost along the way.

Through our calls and *Life Edits* workbook, you'll identify and over-come obstacles blocking your success and happiness. The Editor's Circle will give you a plan and the confidence to take action and turn your dreams into reality.

Using *Life Edits*, we'll dig deep and help you start writing a bold new chapter for your life and career. You'll discover things you should delete that are holding you back, begin inserting ideas and qualities to help you grow, begin moving toward new experiences, and remain true to your authentic self.

Are you ready to be the heroine of your story? Take that step of faith today and join the Editor's Circle. Together, we'll con-nect the dots between your professional and personal dreams, so you can live a life of clarity and reach your successfully ever after.

Join the Editor's Circle. Visit www.chelliephillips.com and sign up today.

Chellie W. Phillips

AUTHOR, SPEAKER, MOTIVATOR

BRING CHELLIE TO YOUR NEXT EVENT

Chellie is a proven speaker on national stages and will encourage your audience to tell their story, remain authentic, expand their influence and find clarity in life.

Start the conversation today.
contact@chelliephillips.com

CPSIA information can be obtained
at www.ICGtesting.com
Printed in the USA
FFHW021403210119
50261102-55247FF